The Order of the Golden Fleece
at Chapel Hill, 1904–2004

G. NICHOLAS HERMAN

The Order of the Golden Fleece
at Chapel Hill, 1904–2004

AMERICA'S FIRST HONOR SOCIETY

FOR UNIVERSITY LEADERS

THE UNIVERSITY OF NORTH CAROLINA AT

CHAPEL HILL LIBRARY · CHAPEL HILL

Designed and typeset by Kachergis Book Design
in Myriad and Walbaum

Manufactured in the United States of America

The paper in this book meets the guidelines for permanence and
durability of the Committee on Production Guidelines for Book Longevity of the
Council on Library Resources.

Distributed by the Bull's Head Bookshop
CB #1530, Daniels Building
UNC–Chapel Hill
Chapel Hill, NC 27599-1530
(919) 962-5060
bullshead@store.unc.edu

LIBRARY OF CONGRESS CATALOGING-IN-PUBLICATION DATA

Herman, G. Nicholas.
The Order of the Golden Fleece at Chapel Hill, 1904–2004 : America's
first honor society for university leaders / G. Nicholas Herman.
p. cm.
Includes bibliographical references and index.
ISBN 0-9721600-4-3 (alk. paper)
1. Order of the Golden Fleece (University of North Carolina)   I. Title.
LJ85.O73H47 2005
378.56'56--dc22
                                                                    2005016843

CLOTH   08   07   06   05   04   5   4   3   2   1

Contents

Illustrations

Preface

THIS BOOK WAS WRITTEN at the request of the Centennial Planning Committee of the Order of the Golden Fleece as part of the order's centennial observance, which was held at the University of North Carolina at Chapel Hill on March 26–27, 2004.[1] Its aim is to provide a reliable account of the origins, ideals, traditions, and work of the order within and for the university over the past one hundred years.[2]

Writing a history of the order was first considered in 1922, but nothing came of the idea then.[3] In 1950, Fleece member William Robert Coulter wrote the order's first history, commonly called "the Gold Book" due to the color of its cover. It was a confidential work, "not to be seen or read by any persons except members [of the Order]."[4] The accuracy of Coulter's work, particularly its account of the origins of the Fleece, was hampered by the dearth of available records. He did not have the benefit of the order's first minute books of 1904–1911 and 1913–1927, for example, because these and other documents were not accessible to members of the order—and largely unknown to them—until 1987, when the order arranged for the University Archives at Louis Round Wilson Library to serve as the official repository for all of its records. At that time, the order's faculty advisor donated materials that had long been kept in his home to the archive.[5] In light of the discovery of these records by the order's members, the Centennial Committee believed that a new history of the Fleece was warranted in order to set out what is now known about the true origins of the order and to provide a full account of the order's endeavors during its entire first century.

The Centennial Committee also believed that, unlike the Gold Book, the new history should be made public. This decision is in keeping with the unmistakable intent of the founding members, who deliberately sought to publicize the ideals and objectives of the order.[6] It is also consistent with the status of the Fleece as the most prestigious honorary society at the university and the first university leadership honorary society in the nation. The history of the order has become an integral part of the history of the university and of the broader history of university honor societies in the country. Accordingly, the active order formally adopted a resolution authorizing the writing and publication of this book.[7]

The author gratefully acknowledges the willing assistance of the following members of the order, who reviewed the manuscript and made valuable editorial and substantive contributions to this book: Doris Waugh Betts, Thomas Kevin B. Cherry, Frank Weston "Westy" Fenhagen, Douglass Hunt, George Lensing Jr., John Lassiter Sanders, Willis Padgett "Bill" Whichard, and Edwin Milton Yoder Jr. The appendices to the book were selflessly prepared by Fleece members Rebecca Susanne Williford, Ashton Lee Wheeler, and Eleanor Saunders Morris. The author also thanks Judith Panitch, research and special projects librarian at the University of North Carolina at Chapel Hill Library, for her invaluable assistance in the production of this work.

The Order of the Golden Fleece
at Chapel Hill, 1904–2004

Prologue

Having dared to surpass the many, you sought the golden fleece.

—Motto of the Order of the Golden Fleece

IN ANCIENT TIMES, Jason, a young man of twenty years, had been brought up in exile by the good centaur Chiron, who taught him virtue and the arts of chivalry. Chiron himself was the very model of the good tutor. He had also guided Achilles, Hercules, and the great physician Asclepius. In his instruction, he drew young heroes aside temporarily from the dangers and corruptions of the society from which they came and helped them to develop the knowledge and character that would enable them to return in time and assume their responsibilities.

Jason was the rightful heir to the throne of a kingdom in Thessaly, but his father had been cruelly deposed by his brother, and Jason had been exiled. The usurping king had been warned by an oracle to "beware of the man with one sandal." Jason, carrying a helpless old woman across a river, lost one sandal as he struggled through the mud. The old woman he carried was in fact the goddess Hera in disguise, however, and she recognized his chivalry and kindness. She promised him her aid in his future life.

When Jason claimed his kingdom from the usurper, the king answered that the realm would be restored to Jason's rule only if the young man could first bring home the golden fleece from the great golden ram that had soared across the heavens. The golden fleece, guarded by a fierce dragon, was in the Kingdom of Colchis, a perilous sea voyage away.

Jason took up the challenge and immediately began building a ship that he called the *Argo*. He gathered a band of fifty men to make the journey with him. Jason and his Argonauts set sail across the Black Sea toward Colchis on a voyage that lasted many years. Trials and obstacles beset them at every step, constantly testing their courage, endurance, and resolve.

The final, greatest obstacle was the Clashing Rocks, two giant boulders that were hurled together by the force of the wind, blocking the way of all vessels seeking to pass. No ship had succeeded in sailing safely between them. But the sage Phineus advised Jason to release a dove; if the dove succeeded in flying between the rocks, the Argonauts should row swiftly in pursuit. Jason released the dove, the Argonauts bent mightily to their oars, and, with the help of the goddess Hera, the *Argo* just managed to escape being crushed between the Clashing Rocks.

Arriving in Colchis, Jason confronted the king and asked for the golden fleece. The king assented, but he set what he considered an almost impossible condition for releasing the fleece to Jason. The young man had to yoke a pair of fire-breathing bulls and with them plough a large field, sow it with dragon's teeth, and then slay the armed men who would spring up from the dragon's teeth, and who would try to take his life in battle. Undaunted, Jason accepted the king's terms. He was aided by Medea, the king's daughter, who had fallen in love with him through Hera's influence. Choosing Jason over her own family, Medea gave him a magic charm to protect him as he performed his allotted tasks.

When the armed men sprang up and rushed upon Jason, he cast a stone among them, and they fell upon each other. Lulling the guardian dragon to sleep with a potion given to him by Medea, Jason seized the dazzling golden fleece. With Medea and his Argonauts, he escaped the vengeful king of Colchis and sailed home to his own land, becoming its rightful king.[1]

CHAPTER ONE

The Turn of the Twentieth Century

THE FOUNDING of the Order of the Golden Fleece in the spring of 1904, as the University of North Carolina entered the second decade of its second century, was an appropriate milestone and marker. For the university stood on the threshold of its transformation from a provincial college to a university of national rank.

A signal figure in the founding of the order was Professor Henry Horace Williams, a legendary teacher of philosophy at Chapel Hill from 1891 until the eve of World War II. Many tales are told of Williams, a self-described Hegelian who addressed his students as "my boys" and was called by them "Horace" behind his back.[1] Albert Coates, who became a Fleece member in 1917 and later founded the university's School of Government, recalled, "Professor Williams never tried to tell us what to think; he tried to see what we did think—our own thoughts and nobody else's. He wanted to see us take flame and blaze with fires we ourselves generated." Coates explained that Williams encouraged his students to work doggedly on problems until they had the "Eureka experience" of discovering its answer in a "moment of insight." Williams taught students to make facts "dynamic" by putting them into a "working relationship," creating a "'whole' greater than the sum of all its parts."[2] Argonaut Thomas Wolfe made Horace a character in *Look Homeward, Angel*.[3] "We boys didn't know what the Old Man taught," Wolfe wrote, "and we didn't give a damn. He taught us to think and that was enough. He was the Hegel of the Cotton Patch."[4]

In early April 1904, two of Professor Williams's boys, Roach Sidney Stewart and Robert Withington Herring, sat down with him to think.[5] They were first-year law students, having received their bachelor of philosophy degrees at the university the preceding spring. As undergraduates, both had been prizewinning debaters in the school's prestigious Dialectic and Philanthropic literary societies—Stewart for the "Di" and Herring for the "Phi." Stewart had otherwise distinguished himself as captain of the football team, and Herring had been the associate editor of both the *Tar Heel*—the campus newspaper—and the *University Magazine*.[6] As student leaders, they were concerned about the pervasive factionalism that plagued the university of their day. Hoping to come up with a dramatic solution to the problem, they said to Professor Williams, "Let us do something."[7]

After conferring with Williams, Stewart and Herring decided to convene a meeting of student leaders in the professor's office on April 11, 1904.[8] The plan was to bring together in one setting those students who best represented the eight principal branches of university life, which at the time included debating, scholarship, publications, writing, athletics, religious life, professional and graduate student life, and social life (represented by the "typical University man").[9] They invited six seniors: Sidney Swain Robins, debater for the Di and president of both the senior class and the scholastic honorary society, Alpha Theta Phi; Charles

Henry Horace Williams, charter Argonaut and faculty advisor (North Carolina Collection, Louis Round Wilson Library, University of North Carolina at Chapel Hill)

Phillips Russell, editor-in-chief of the *Tar Heel* and the *University Magazine;* William Picard Jacocks and Albert Lyman Cox, athletes on the varsity football team; Alfred Williams Haywood Jr., a "typical University man" who was class secretary, essayist, and manager of the senior track team; and Ralph Moore Harper, president of the YMCA.[10] Stewart (who was president of the law class)[11] and Herring represented the professional school sector of the student body. Out of this meeting, the Golden Fleece was born.

For most of its first century since opening its doors on January 15, 1795, the university, whose student comity the new order was founded to serve, had been a small, provincial college struggling for its mere existence. Although the North Carolina General Assembly's chartering legislation of December 11, 1789, called for a public university that would be "supported by permanent funds and well endowed," regular state appropriations were nonexistent until 1881.[12] For decades, the university faced periodic attacks from private denominational colleges and other political forces that railed against the "godless" institution. From 1871 to 1875, it was completely shut down due to the political and economic upheavals of the Civil War and its aftermath. By the end of the 1800s, however, these struggles were beginning to subside, and a groundswell of support for public education arose throughout the state. In this new climate, the first public university in the nation was poised to begin its steady ascent to national prominence.

In June 1900, President Francis Preston Venable, a professor of chemistry and one of the first Ph.D.s on the faculty, became the university's thirteenth presiding officer. He declared that the "heart and soul of an education institution lies in its teaching force," and his vision was to build "a large body of strong, trained men, eminent scholars, skillful investigators, inspiring teachers."[13] In the first two years of his administration, he added over a dozen new faculty members, among them a young English instructor, Edward Kidder Graham, who succeeded Venable as president in 1914.[14] Venable reorganized the structure of the university by grouping related departments of instruction into separate schools, placing each under a dean. To the existing schools of law, medicine, and pharmacy he added the College of Liberal Arts, the Graduate School, the Summer School, the School of Mines (later called Applied Sciences), and the School of Pedagogy (Education). To oversee the entire academic program, he appointed as dean of the faculty Eben Alexander, a professor of Greek language and literature.[15] By the 1902–1903 academic year, there were 575 students and 64 faculty members at the university. This made it one of the largest in the South, far surpassing the University of Virginia, Vanderbilt University, and Tulane University in student body size and teaching force.[16]

Chapel Hill at the time was a small village nestled in a bucolic wilderness. These were horse and buggy days. At the beginning of the school year, local students arrived on campus by horseback or carriage. Those from farther away arrived by train at Carrboro and hired a carriage for fifty cents to take them and their meager belongings up the hill to campus. Franklin Street, the heart of the village, "was a dusty red avenue cut through a forest of magnificent trees,"[17] and what is now Cameron Avenue, running through the center of campus, was nothing more than a dirt path. Except for the land cleared for buildings, the university and the rustic village were surrounded by forest.

Life on campus, though somewhat primitive, had a special ambience of down-home charm and intimacy. Although there was heating and a water and sewer system, there was no hot water in the dormitories. Bathing and toilet facilities were located in Law

Sub, the basement of Smith Hall (the building that was later to become Playmakers Theatre), and Bynum Gymnasium.[18] Because roughly three-fourths of the students lived barely above the "bread and butter line," many had part-time jobs as waiters, dishwashers, or clerks in downtown stores—whatever work they could find to help make ends meet.[19] Some even maintained barbershops or shoe shops in their rooms or served as agents for out-of-town men's clothing establishments.[20] Given the isolation of the campus and the small student body, the intimate relationships students forged among themselves often extended to close bonds between students and their faculty mentors.

The university was also very much a man's world. Women were first admitted in 1897, when five women registered in the junior class. By 1899, three had graduated.[21] But in the early 1900s, there were fewer than ten women students enrolled in any given year. They shared the classroom with their male counterparts but lived in private houses off campus.[22] Women would not attain full membership in campus life and organizations for many decades.[23]

The majority of students were undergraduates, and the academic requirements for admission and graduation were rigorous. Studies in the freshmen and sophomore years included Greek and Latin along with English, history, mathematics, French, German, and physics.[24] Students who had not had the good fortune of attending a private secondary school were often greatly disadvantaged, because few public high schools in the state were equipped to prepare students adequately for college work. Consequently, the "academic mortality rate" was extremely high.[25] In the early 1900s, less than 30 percent of those who entered the university as freshmen graduated.[26]

For those students who survived—academically and financially—the intellectual life of the campus extended well beyond the classroom. At the center of this extracurricular intellectualism were the Philanthropic and Dialectic literary societies, which were as old as the university itself. Robert Burton House, who became a Fleece member as a student in 1915 and was later chancellor of the Chapel Hill campus, explained that a single society had been founded along with the university in 1795 but that it had "at once" divided into two societies that competed "primarily in debate, but also for every other University honor." Every student was required to join one of the literary societies, and they customarily divided along the lines of geography, with students from eastern North Carolina becoming members of the Phi and those from the west joining the Di.

In 1859, New East and New West halls were constructed for the Phi and the Di, respectively. These buildings were "handsomely furnished and decorated by the societies and were said to be the most elegant in America" at the time of their dedication. Society proceedings, too, were elegant, as House recalled: "It was an inspiration to see the president and the subordinate officers seated behind mahogany desks on the rostrum with the society insignia on the background wall, facing a room full of members seated in a semi-circular arrangement of scroll-work iron chairs upholstered in red."

The literary societies assumed an educational role, as the university's literary instruction focused on Greek and Latin to the detriment of English and modern foreign languages. They purchased books and gave their members weekly reading and writing assignments. The latter "were read to the society and rigidly criticized by elected officers." But the bulk of the societies' energies were devoted to public speaking, which was seen as "direct preparation for law and politics in the young republic" and thus "practical professional training for public life." House reminisced, "More men went out for debating than for football in those days, and the Debater's Monogram was the most coveted award in the University." In sum, "No student who aspired to leadership could afford to neglect the most powerful student organization; nor did such a student want to miss the personal development and the fun."[27]

Though the Phi and Di took center stage, the Elisha Mitchell Scientific Society, the Shakespeare Club, the North Carolina Historical Society, the Geological Journal, the Chemical Club, and the Philological Club all had their place in campus life in the early 1900s. The Alpha Theta Phi Society was founded on the campus in 1894 "to stimulate and increase a desire for sound scholarship" and was merged into the university's chapter of Phi Beta Kappa when it was established on September 7, 1904.[28]

The university yearbook, the *Yackety Yack,* called all of these societies the "Non-Frat Organizations." Other such organizations, which were mostly social in nature, included the freshman society, Pi Sigma; the sophomore societies, Theta Nu Epsilon and Order of Sphinx; the junior societies, the Gorgon's Head and the Order of Gimghouls; a legal society, Omega Tau; and two other societies about which little is now known, the One and the Yi. There was also the German Club, a dance club that chose the leaders of the fall, Easter, and commencement dances. Religious life centered upon the Young Men's Christian Association, which was one of the largest non-frat organizations on campus.[29] Along with the *Yackety Yack,* the principal student publications were the *University Magazine* and the *Tar Heel,* which did not become a daily until 1929.[30]

As distinguished from the non-frat organizations, there were ten social fraternities: Alpha Tau Omega, Beta Theta Pi, Delta Kappa Epsilon, Kappa Alpha, Kappa Sigma, Phi Delta Theta, Pi Kappa Alpha, Sigma Alpha Epsilon, Sigma Nu, and Zeta Psi.[31] Students who did not belong to any of these fraternities were known as "non-frats," and they comprised approximately three-fourths of the student body. The non-frats outnumbered the "frats" three or four to one in the Phi and Di and excelled at least as well as the frats in scholarship, debating, commencement honors, and athletics.[32]

Over time, a deep division developed between the frats and the non-frats, a schism that became a sort of "rivalry of the haves and have-nots."[33] The two groups fiercely competed over the election of class officers, commencement marshals, and positions on student publications with a "partisanship as bitter as you can find in a New York ward election."[34] While the frats dominated the editorial positions for the *Tar Heel*, the non-frats controlled the editorships of the *University Magazine*. For a short time in 1894, the non-frats even established their own newspaper, the *White and Blue*, in protest over the *Tar Heel*'s excessive featuring of athletics to the exclusion of other university activities. Hostilities between fraternity men and non-fraternity men extended among the classes as well, inspiring, in particular, the constant hazing of freshmen by upperclassmen.[35] There was no formal structure of campuswide student self-government, and although the prestigious literary societies attempted to regulate the behavior of their members through various rules and regulations, their efforts to bring unity to the campus were largely unsuccessful. Thus, when Venable became president in 1900, "student government probably posed more difficulties [for him] than any other phase of University life."[56] The otherwise intimate campus environment was fractured by a pervasive atmosphere of division, factionalism, and disharmony.

On April 11, 1904, this was about to change for the better. The new order founded by Stewart and Herring at Professor Williams's office that evening was to become a vital ingredient in the shaping of the university's twentieth-century character.

CHAPTER 2

From the Templars to the Order of the Golden Fleece

ALONG WITH HORACE WILLIAMS, Professor Edward Kidder Graham was invited to join the organization at its inaugural meeting in the capacity of faculty advisor. In the 1903–1904 academic year, Graham was an associate professor of English.[1] As a student at the university from 1894 to 1898, he had been ranked second in his class, had performed as a brilliant debater for the Di, and had devoted himself to baseball and tennis.[2] Professor Williams considered Graham to be the best student he had ever taught.[3] Fleeceman Albert Coates, who called Professor Graham "the greatest man that I have known and worked with in flesh and blood upon this earth,"[4] spoke of Graham's special relationship with students: "By asserting that students were able and good, he helped make them able and good—inspired them to be better than they were. . . . He never sought to dominate or overawe, or subdue anyone, but to make every man his own master. . . . The men associated with him felt, not that they were working for him, but that he was giving to them a medium and opportunity for doing in the biggest way the thing they wanted to do. Around him men felt free."[5]

At the meeting, the band of eight students and two faculty advisors discussed "the matter of organizing a Senior Class society which should subordinate local interests to the welfare of the University and join together in closer harmony the different branches of [campus] life."[6] With this objective in mind, the group met again on April 12 and 14. At these meetings, the fledgling society adopted a constitution prepared by Alfred Haywood and Professor Graham and appointed committees to propose a name and appropriate colors. It also elected its first officers: Alfred Haywood, president; Sidney Robins, vice-president; Albert Cox, secretary; and Ralph Harper, treasurer.[7]

On April 16, the new society elected Eben Alexander, dean of the faculty, as a third faculty advisor.[8] Before becoming chair of Greek at the university in 1886, Dean Alexander had been a professor of Greek and chairman of the faculty at the University of Tennessee. From 1893 to 1897, he served as minister to Greece under the administration of President Grover Cleveland, and in that capacity he was instrumental in the revival of the Olympic Games.[9] Because Dean Alexander was the senior academic officer of the university, his membership in the society meant that it gained a voice at the highest levels of the administration.

During ensuing April meetings, the society made its membership more representative of the university community by electing as charter members two additional seniors—Neill Ray Graham, editor-in-chief of the *Yackety Yack*, and William Fisher, an accomplished varsity football player—as well as a graduate student, William Jones Gordon, who provided appropriate representation from the Graduate School.[10] Most important, the society's members decided to call themselves "the Templars."[11]

The original Templars—or "the Knights Templar," as they were more formally known—were a monastic military order

Edward Kidder Graham, charter Argonaut and faculty advisor (North Carolina Collection, Louis Round Wilson Library, University of North Carolina at Chapel Hill)

Eben Alexander, charter Argonaut and faculty advisor (North Carolina Collection, Louis Round Wilson Library, University of North Carolina at Chapel Hill)

founded by a small cadre of French knights in Jerusalem in 1118 at the end of the First Crusade. As both monks and knights, their responsibility was to protect Christian pilgrims to the Holy Land. Many believe the warrior monks formed the first chivalric order in the world, which became the prototype for all subsequent orders of knighthood. With the backing of the Holy See and the European monarchies, the Templars amassed considerable wealth and political power over two centuries. In 1307, however, the king of France, Philip the Fair, who was indebted to the Templars and felt threatened by their political power, arrested all known Templars; he burned their last grand master at the stake in 1314. For nearly four centuries thereafter, remnants of the Templars remained underground. The order regained public standing in 1705 when France's Duke of Orleans was elected grand master. By the mid-1800s, the order had revitalized itself and reached the peak of its prominence, with chapters spread throughout Europe and Africa as well as in India, Brazil, and New York City.[12]

Having adopted the name of this prestigious and ancient society, the fourteen knights of the university's Templars continued the process of organizing themselves by discussing suitable society regalia, the design of a badge, and potential induction ceremonies for current and prospective members. But, having second thoughts about the name they had chosen for the society, they soon adopted a motion to reconsider it at a later meeting. They also decided that once a final name had been agreed upon a notice would be sent to state newspapers and the *Tar Heel* to announce the formation and purposes of the new society.[13] In May, with commencement one month away, the Templars elected eight new members from the junior class to carry the society forward into the next academic year and inducted them into the society on May 14.[14]

Meanwhile, on May 3, the Templars unanimously voted to change the society's name to "the Order of the Golden Fleece" and to adopt white and gold as the order's colors. Albert Cox's minutes from that meeting do not explain why the society decided to change its name,[15] but it is reasonable to assume that the members were more comfortable with the image of the Golden Fleece, drawn as it was from a famous legend grounded in the ancient classics that they had studied so thoroughly, than with that of a French chivalric order.

At the time, there were only two other Orders of the Golden Fleece in the world. Philip the Good, Duke of Burgundy, established the first in 1430. In 1477, the order was passed to the house of Hapsburg, and it continued under the Spanish branch of the Hapsburgs. The initial Spanish investiture occurred in 1519, and in 1700 Phillip V and Ferdinand VI united the order to the crown of Spain. In 1712, however, the house of Austria reclaimed the order from Spain, with the result that thereafter there were two Orders of the Golden Fleece, one conferred by the Austrian monarch and the other by the Spanish monarch.[16]

The members of the university order held six additional meetings in May devoted to completing organizational details before the summer recess. They decided to call the president of the order "O Mighty Jason," the vice-president "vice-Jason," the secretary "grammateus," and the treasurer "Chrystopher." (The active order in 1949–1950 changed "vice-Jason" to "hyparchos," which means "vice-regent" or "lieutenant" in Greek.) Members of the order were to be called "Argonauts." The constitution was amended to provide that in future years new Argonauts would be selected on April 15 and initiated on May 1. Also, to commemorate the new order, the student founders had themselves photographed.[17]

The last meeting in the spring of 1904 was held on May 28.

The charter student Argonauts. *Bottom row, left to right,* William Picard Jacocks, Ralph Moore Harper, Charles Phillips Russell, Albert Lyman Cox, and Alfred Williams Haywood Jr. *Top row, left to right,* Robert Withington Herring, Roach Sidney Stewart, Sidney Swain Robins, William Jones Gordon, William Fisher, and Neill Ray Graham. (North Carolina Collection, Louis Round Wilson Library, University of North Carolina at Chapel Hill)

This meeting was attended by the eight new Argonauts. Professor Williams gave a talk about the ideals and objectives of the order, and he was asked to prepare an article about the origins and purposes of the Fleece for the summer edition of the *Tar Heel*.[18] The article, which Albert Cox described as giving "an excellent insight into the origins of the Order of the Golden Fleece,"[19] also offers insight into the motivations that led to the society's founding and is worth quoting at length:

> In the old life at Chapel Hill there was signal unity and a consequent pervading enthusiasm for every University interest. . . . But things changed. Our life divided. Many local interests supplanted the old unity of University life. This produced friction and harshness—oftentimes ugliness in the student life. The thoughtful men saw the facts and grieved over the situation. They talked—and planned—and hoped. But the facts would not change. Every suggestion seemed to fall away and die without fruit.
>
> At last the token of a better day has come. The students throughout the University have set themselves to the task. It has been the deepest question in college life this year. The strong men and true men worked together. And we have closed the year in a clear conviction that an advance has been made.
>
> As we saw it, the problem was to restore unity to college life. . . . we agreed that if the leading men in the Senior class could be banded together in strong bonds the result would follow. That is, supposing that there are eight lines of permanent interest and work in the University; then take the best man in each of these lines of activity and bind them together. This will create mutual respect and admiration and therefore give a basis for college unity. And college unity is the absolute condition of college achievement and enthusiasm.
>
> . . . And the Golden Fleece was organized. The idea became clear and a deep feeling of satisfaction [arose] once a beginning had been made. Good things for University life must follow.

When the leaders of college life in all its interests are brought together, each must come to know the strength of the other and be helped. Thus a larger view of life must prevail here and a deeper, broader sympathy. Artificial standards must go. Narrow medieval habits of feeling will wither and die. Deep, broad and magnificent must be the flow of University life. True, and good and beautiful must be the typical University man. For all the forces in our life work together for him in eternal unity and peace. This is the ideal of the Golden Fleece.[20]

Thus, the Golden Fleece was born. It sought unity in the face of division—an earthly goal inspired by belief in a broader universal order characterized by eternal harmony and peace. Over the next hundred years, the society's task was to make that goal a reality for the greater good of the university and in the lives of all who served and loved it.

The First University Honorary Society of Its Kind in the Nation

THE PUBLICATION of Professor Williams's article in the *Tar Heel* was the first of a series of deliberate efforts by the early Argonauts to record publicly the origins and objectives of the newly founded order for the students of their day and future generations. The order introduced itself in the 1904–1905 *Student Handbook* published by the YMCA as "a senior organization of the varied interests of student life." "Just as the Alpha Theta Phi picks out the best scholars," the description explained, "so the Golden Fleece brings together men who have made marked distinction in University life, provided there is a corresponding symmetry in the other phases of their life."[1]

Thereafter, beginning in 1906, the order regularly publicized itself in the *Yackety Yack*, a practice that continues to this day. In the 1908 edition, Professor Edward Kidder Graham was called upon again to summarize the organization's purposes, and he explained that the group "was not sectional, social, athletic, or scholarly—it sought to bring together the best from the whole." By doing so, the order attempted "to present a composite picture of the University man." Its business, he said, "was to discuss University affairs in a liberal mood of sympathy, to make a constructive council that would summarize the loyal intent of representative citizens to do whatever might be done to foster the general good." Concluding by putting the order in a national context, Graham wrote: "This is the meaning of The Golden Fleece. It is a part of the University Movement—a feeling of national consciousness that I believe is now the dominating mood of the college."[2]

In the November 1913 issue of the *University Magazine,* Argonaut John S. Cansler reported the strides the society had made in the first nine years of its existence. "From its nature," he explained, the Fleece had acted more as "an influence than a visible physical agent." But it had been an effective influence: "Not perfect yet—and never will be for that matter—we may nevertheless feel proud of our progress. Politics have gone. . . . Factions have lost, first, their bitterness; then largely their being. Lines of division are being dimmed. Consciously or unconsciously we are coming to realize the utter uselessness of factional feelings and the very littleness of fraternity prejudice. When we do that we have advanced tremendously."[3]

In light of these concerted efforts to provide a public record of the order's origins and purposes, it is ironic that for most of the twentieth century the true origins of the order became shrouded in myths that were unwittingly reported by four university historians, all of whom were members of the Fleece.[4] In 1950, William Robert Coulter selflessly wrote the first history of the order, *The History of the Golden Fleece,* commonly called "the Gold Book" due to the color of its cover. Based on interviews with five of the founding Argonauts, Coulter reported that the order was founded in 1903; that "the thought of the Fleece first had lodgment in the mind of Dr. Eben Alexander, who was a member of Skull and Bones at Yale"; that the initial meeting of the founding members was held in Professor Alexander's office; and that the plan for the order was "somewhat similar to that of the Skull and Bones at Yale."[5] Seven years later, Louis Round Wilson published *The University of North Carolina, 1900–1930: The Making of a Modern University.* Wilson, too, reported that the order was founded in 1903, and he went on to say that it was organized by Professors Alexander, Williams, and Graham, rather than by student leaders.[6] Robert B. House and William D. Snider repeated very similar claims in histories published in 1964 and 1992, respectively.[7]

Based on these accounts, it became conventional wisdom among the members of the order that the society had been established in 1903 when Professor Alexander, with the assistance of Professors Williams and Graham, came up with the idea, modeling it after Yale University's Skull and Bones Society, of which he had been a member.[8] Thus, it was proclaimed that the order was "second only to the Skull and Bones at Yale and its competitive groups there as first in the field of honorary societies on American college campuses."[9]

It is now known, however, that these accounts were mistaken. The order's first minute book of 1904–1911, which contains Albert Cox's detailed account of the fourteen meetings in April and May of 1904 at which the order was conceived and organized, unmistakably shows that the idea for it came not from Professor Alexander but from Roach Stewart and Robert Herring in their initial conference with Professor Williams. Before Professor Alexander was even elected to join the new society, it had already held three meetings at which the original band of eight student leaders — along with their faculty advisors, Professors Williams and Graham—had adopted a constitution, taken steps to come up with a name for the order, and elected officers. When Professor Alexander was elected as the third faculty advisor, the society was called the Templars. As the minutes make clear, the order was founded by students to "join together in closer harmony the different branches of [University] life,"[10] not by autocratic faculty members who wished to exhort students to higher academic attainment. The personal and pedagogical relationship that Professors Williams, Graham, and Alexander had with their students, moreover, was never an autocratic one, but rather one designed, as Coates put it, to make students "think," to make them feel "free."[11] Skull and Bones is not mentioned anywhere in Cox's minutes, in any subsequent minutes of the order, or in any of the articles or announcements that the early Argonauts published about the order's origins and purposes. Although it is true that Professor Alexander was a member of Skull and Bones and personally likened his membership in the Fleece to his college days as a "Bonesman,"[12] there is nothing in the record about the founding of the Fleece to support the view that it was modeled on Skull and Bones.

This is not to say that the accounts given by Coulter, Wilson, House, and Snider were irresponsibly reported. They wrote from the best information available to them. But more information was forthcoming. Argonaut Joseph Maryon Saunders, for forty-three years the university's alumni secretary, had for many years hosted meetings of the active order in his home or office when he was its faculty advisor. Aware of how easily records of student activities can be lost, he had quietly preserved a careful Golden Fleece file, including the order's first minute books of 1904–1911 and 1913–1927, which for many years were stored in the attic of his home.[13] Argonaut Robert Edward Johnson, elected Jason in 1982, worked with university archivist Michael G. Martin to establish a Fleece archive in the university's archives accessible only to members of the order. Learning of this project, Saunders arranged for the orderly transfer of the early records to the new archive in 1987.[14] Even then, however, the true history of the origins of the order was not appreciated until 2001, when the first minute books were examined by members of the order in connection with research being conducted for the Centennial Committee in preparation for the order's centennial celebration—which was not held in 2003, as initially planned, but instead was moved to 2004 in light of the discovery.[15]

The fact that the Golden Fleece was not modeled after Skull and Bones is significant in a larger historical context. The first college honor society in the nation, Phi Beta Kappa, was founded on December 5, 1776, at the College of William and Mary in Williamsburg, Virginia.[16] In its early years, Phi Beta Kappa was essentially a debating and literary club "formed for congeniality and to promote good fellowship, with 'friendship as its basis and benevolence and literature as its pillars.'"[17] The first branch of the society was established at Yale on November 13, 1780. By 1900, Phi Beta Kappa was exclusively an academic honor society, and the society's Chapel Hill chapter was formed on September 7, 1904, absorbing the university's existing scholastic society, Alpha Theta Phi.[18]

Meanwhile, in the early 1830s, a Yale student named William H. Russell went to study for a year in Germany, where he befriended the leader of a secret society "that hailed the death's head as its logo."[19] Returning to Yale for the 1832–1833 academic year, Russell became incensed with Phi Beta Kappa when it failed to elect to its ranks a prominent undergraduate scholar, Eleazar

Kingsbury Foster. Otherwise disenchanted with the quality of the Yale faculty and angered that Phi Beta Kappa had been stripped of its status as a secret society, in December 1832 Russell enlisted Foster and thirteen other students to form a new secret society that was to become Skull and Bones, formally named the "Brotherhood of Death."[20] The true purpose of Skull and Bones, then and today, is not altogether clear. The society is extraordinarily secret, its members pledging never to reveal its affairs. But at bottom, it is largely a fraternal organization, providing its members with a distinguished circle of colleagues with whom to network and build lasting relationships.

Except for the fact that many members of both Skull and Bones and the Golden Fleece have lived lives of distinguished service to their communities, their nation, and the world, there are no meaningful parallels between the two societies.[21] The 1913 Constitution of the order stated that its purpose was "to stimulate its members to a full realization of the highest ideals of University life, and to bring about through organization a closer unity of the forces of University life,"[22] whereas Skull and Bones was not established for any such purpose.

The Fleece has also never practiced secrecy in the same way that secrecy has characterized the special culture of Skull and Bones. Consistent with the purpose of the Fleece, the fundamental criteria for membership—"outstanding personal integrity, a superlative record of achievement and service, and loyalty to the University"[23]—are well known. But there are no clear criteria for becoming a Bonesman. The privacy of Fleece affairs is deliberately designed to promote frank and free discussion among its members about ways to better the university community and to allow them to effect those betterments through quiet, individual endeavors, free from the imprimatur of a formal interest group. For Skull and Bones, however, uncompromising secrecy is primarily designed to foster and preserve a sacred sense of communality and brotherhood. And whereas the symbol of Skull and Bones represents a mystical symbiosis between mortality and fraternity, the symbol of the Golden Fleece represents a special quest for unity, harmony, and service.

The oldest university honor society resembling the Golden Fleece is Omicron Delta Kappa, founded ten years after the Fleece on December 3, 1914, at Washington and Lee University in Lexington, Virginia. Although ODK's origins and purposes are strikingly similar to those of the Fleece, there is no evidence that the ODK founders knew about the Chapel Hill order.[24] ODK was founded by twelve student leaders and three faculty advisors with "the idea that leadership of exceptional quality and versatility in college should be recognized, that representatives in all phases of college life should cooperate in a worthwhile endeavor, and that outstanding students, faculty and administration members should meet on a basis of mutual interest, understanding and helpfulness."

In words reminiscent of those of Professor Graham and Argonaut Cansler, Rupert N. Latture, one of the founding student members of ODK, explained: "We agreed that our purpose was to weld the campus leaders into a constructive force for service on the campus. To insure that no one segment of the student body would dominate the group, provision was made for the selection of members to be distributed among five divisions based on leadership in scholarship, athletics, publications, public speaking and social and religious activities. Members were to be chosen from the junior and senior classes. . . . We agreed that there should be included in active membership a limited number of faculty members who would serve as advisors and provide continuity."[25]

In time, Omicron Delta Kappa expanded into a national leadership honor society and established its headquarters at the University of Kentucky in Lexington, Kentucky. In 1926 and 1932, the Golden Fleece was invited to join the organization, but it declined.[26] By the turn of the twenty-first century, ODK had chapters—or "circles," as the society calls them—at nearly three hundred universities and colleges in the United States, including the University of North Carolina campuses at Charlotte, Asheville, Wilmington, Greenville, and Boone.[27]

This history of the origins and purposes of Phi Beta Kappa, Skull and Bones, and Omicron Delta Kappa reveals that the Order of the Golden Fleece was the first university honorary society of its kind in the nation.

CHAPTER FOUR

Only the Best

FROM THE ORDER'S EARLIEST DAYS, its purposes and criteria for membership were constitutionally grounded. The first constitutions of 1904 and 1913 prescribed that the order's "object shall be to stimulate its members to a full realization of the highest ideals of University life, and to bring about through organization a closer unity of the forces of University life."[1] The 1913 Constitution set out the qualifications for membership as follows: "[A member] must be a man who has shown himself to be of unimpeachable character, loyal to the University and to be possessed of such personal qualifications as to make him worthy of the description: 'a representative University man'; he shall have attained marked distinction in scholarship, or athletics, or literary production, or forensics, or be a man distinguished among his fellow students for a combination of such qualities as give him unquestioned popularity and prominence." In addition, membership was not to be guaranteed to individuals on the basis of their belonging to any particular "team or board or any single achievement of merit," nor was it to be "determined by personal caprice," by friendship, or by "any affiliation of any sort."[2]

More than three-quarters of a century later, the 1994 Constitution combined the order's purposes and qualifications for membership in this way: "The purpose of The Order of the Golden Fleece is to recognize and exemplify in its membership outstanding personal integrity, a superlative record of achievement and in service, and loyalty to The University of North Carolina at Chapel Hill. . . . The public recognition of those students who meet the Order's high standards is intended both to honor those chosen and to establish membership in the Order as a visible and desirable goal that will inspire students to strive for excellence."[3]

In keeping with the intent of the founding members to perpetuate the order's purposes by selecting Argonauts who would be active during the academic year, from 1905 to 1920 the order elected approximately eight students each year, drawn mostly from the junior class.[4] From 1911 to 1919, when the university enrolled fewer than a thousand students, the *Tar Heel* simply published a list of the names of the new Argonauts chosen each spring.[5] The newspaper's first front-page article about the order's tapping ceremony appeared in April 1920, when North Carolina governor Thomas Walter Bickett spoke at the event before a large assembly in Gerrard Hall.[6] Beginning in 1921, the *Tar Heel* expanded its reporting on the order, adopting the practice of providing an advance announcement of the spring tapping ceremony and according full coverage to the annual event.[7]

During its first fifteen years, the order was also careful to preserve the continuity of its faculty advisory board. After Professor Eben Alexander's death in 1910, the order invited Marvin Hendrix Stacy, then a professor of mathematics and later dean of the College of Liberal Arts and chairman of the faculty,[8] to serve as an advisor. He declined because he believed that by serving in this role he would be compromising his stance as "a friend of the non-fraternity man."[9] Consequently, in 1913 the order elected to its faculty board Charles Wesley Bain, a professor of Greek who had been inducted as the Fleece's first honorary member the preceding year. Professor Bain died in 1915. Subsequently, Edward Kidder Graham died during the influenza epidemic that struck the campus in 1918.[10] This left Professor Horace Williams as the sole faculty advisor. To fill the two vacancies on the board, the order elected Frank Porter Graham and Francis Foster Bradshaw in 1921.[11] Both had been inducted into the order when they were students, Graham in 1908 and Bradshaw in 1915. Graham, a professor of history, served as the first dean of students beginning in the 1919–1920 academic year and became president of the university in 1930,[12] succeeding President Harry Woodburn Chase, who had been inducted into the Fleece in 1920 as the order's second honorary member. Bradshaw, who succeeded Professor Williams as chairman of the Philosophy Department, became dean of students in 1921, a position he held until the mid-1940s.

After Professor Williams died in 1940, Argonaut Joseph Maryon Saunders, alumni secretary of the university, served as advisor to the order. In the mid-1970s, Argonaut Charles Franklin Miller, a popular campus housing administrator and counselor of students under the Division of Student Affairs, was chosen for the role. From 1979 to the present, Argonaut George Lensing Jr., professor of English, has served as faculty advisor.

Consistent with its constitutional mandate to select only those students of the highest distinction and character, by 1922 the Fleece had established itself as an honor society of unparalleled prestige in the university community. In that year, the *Tar Heel* described membership in the order as "the most coveted honor to which a Carolina student is eligible" and said that its members "represent the pick of the campus and will be known as the unchallenged champions in their own particular activities."[13] The article went on to opine about the quality of existing "Fleece material" on campus and to speculate about particular students who might be tapped into the order. This type of journalistic speculation continued until 1933, when the newspaper—then a daily—announced in an editorial that it felt "that to continue this policy of mentioning possible candidates would be to jeopardize, for the sake of a news story, the respect which the student body has for the Golden Fleece."[14] But the newspaper continued to give front-page coverage to the new Argonauts selected each spring, and beginning in the 1980s it routinely published the citations given to new members for the achievements that led to their induction into the order.

The prestige of the order eventually exposed it to satire. In the spring of 1923, Samuel Buxton Midyette, whom the *Yackety Yack* described as "another one of those rare birds which we insist upon as being the only one of its kind in captivity,"[15] lampooned the Golden Fleece by establishing a fictitious alternative order, the "Gilded Fuz."[16] Writing under the pseudonym "Hay-Shaker," Midyette published his parody of the Fleece in the May 22, 1923, *Tar Heel*, which also carried a respectful front-page story about the new Argonauts chosen that spring. In introducing the Fuz and the selection of its first members, the Hay-Shaker wrote: "That the aims of the Senior Order of the Golden Fleece aren't good and that the operation of its mechanism is nil, not even the most courageous freshman is willing to affirm. It is a nice little organization composed of nice little boys who have nice little aims." But "the factional elements on the campus" had grown to be too fractious for the "nine men" of the order to handle, the article explained, and thus "the rumored split in the Satyrs, the insurrection of the Playmakers, and embittered political machines call forth a new order: that of the Gilded Fuz." Its purpose, too, was to "pour stilling oil on the rough seas of the dispute." Its members, chosen with "the utmost care in judgment," included "eight men and one co-ed." The spoof went on to list the nine persons inducted into the Fuz, along with a citation for each that was couched in verse. The list of picks included "Johnny Foster: Pirate Club; Rising Barrister; Buccaneer; Money Changer," who was described with this verse: 'A pirate's life is the life for me, / A life a-roaming the boundless sea, / From early morn 'til late at night, / It's blood and thunder and fight and might; / Pieces of eight; pieces of eight.'"

The Hay-Shaker's reporting on the Gilded Fuz continued in May 1924,[17] and a public "rapping," or "wrapping," of new "Fuzzies" was held by Midyette and his cohorts that spring. They donned tow sacks over their heads with little pointed ears and conducted a mock induction ceremony during a baseball game at Emerson Stadium. After Midyette graduated in 1924, his parody passed to Hay-Shaker II, whose continuation of the Fuz burlesques died out after the spring of 1925.[18]

This mostly good-natured spoofing of the Fleece was followed by a more serious challenge to the standing of the order. The problem began in the spring of 1926, when the order inducted only four new members (two juniors and two seniors) rather than the complement of ten typical of those years. After the tapping, the *Tar Heel*, which had clearly anticipated a larger number of new inductees, reported in its May 6, 1926, edition that the meager selection was "entirely without precedent . . . and comes not only to blight the hopes and aspirations of ambitious undergraduates but as a startling innovation to the student body." On the editorial page, the paper asserted that "the order made a mistake in not selecting more men, for there is no getting around the fact that more men were eligible." The editorial then leveled an allegation that struck at the heart of one of the order's core principles: "politics—which is supposed to play no part in Fleece selections—made its insidious influence felt this time and the members of the Fleece wouldn't compromise on candidates." The editorial concluded on a more restrained note: "While it is deplored that friction occurred within the Fleece group itself, perhaps it is better that, since it did occur, men were selected on whom there was unanimity of opinion."[19]

The ensuing summer recess provided only a brief hiatus in the controversy. In the fall of 1926, only two of the four Argonauts inducted the previous spring returned to campus. At a meeting on November 21, 1926, the order discussed and then rejected an invitation to join Omicron Delta Kappa.[20] The next day, the order elected to its ranks three new members, all seniors. The minutes of that meeting do not explain why.[21] Although it is possible the order believed that adding new members right away was necessary to thwart the establishment of an ODK chapter on campus, it is more likely it made the decision in an effort to blunt the *Tar Heel*'s criticism of the previous spring's tapping and to provide for a larger number of Argonauts to carry on its business in the remainder of the academic year.[22] On December 3, the three new Argonauts were quietly notified of their selection and told they would take part in the active order effective immediately but that they would not be formally inducted until the spring.[23] When the campus discovered the private tapping a few days later, there was an uproar.

The leader of the furor was David Donald Carroll, assistant editor of the *Tar Heel* and author of a column called "The Driftwood Fire." In reams of copy over the next two months, he advocated that the Golden Fleece be abolished. In his December 7, 1926, column, he argued that the Fleece was ineffectual in pursuit of its goal of binding student leaders together in service to the student body and that it was untrustworthy: "there are too many needs on this campus to trust their care to [Fleece] leaders who require secrecy for their remedies," he explained. Noting that the principal leaders of the student body—its president, the president of the senior class, and the editors of the *Tar Heel* and the *Carolina Magazine*—met frequently to discuss campus problems, he emphasized that none were members of the order. He characterized being tapped for the Fleece as providing "only a flattery title," describing it as a form of "hero-worship" that induced students to participate in campus activities with "break-neck indulgence" for the narrow goal of earning membership in the order rather than for the selfless purpose of bettering the university community. In sum, he proclaimed: "We tolerate no foppish aristocracy of society here as king of men. But here we have in the Golden Fleece an organization unrepresentative, tyrannical, and conducive to idolatry of the cheapest kind. Many think it laughable. To us the show-off is damnable, unworthy today of a master of logic [Professor Horace Williams] as its founder. This day we break the silence and appeal to you of the student body: Will you continue to endure this farce? If you value merit above vanity, send Golden Fleece to the limbo, which holds the glory that was Greece and the grandeur that was Rome. Golden Fleece must go."

The editor of the *Tar Heel*, James Thurmond Madry, weighed in too, but he stopped short of calling for the outright abolition of the order. While he expressed some sympathy for the Fleece's decision to hold an "unheralded tapping"—whether to preempt the formation of a rival honor society on campus or to placate criticism over the previous spring's paltry selection of new Argonauts—he contended that "if the basis for this organization is that it shall include the outstanding men in scholarship, athletics, debating, religion, publications, student government, *et cetera*, then the Fleece has lost its reason for existing as an honor body." Acknowledging that the three new seniors elected to the order were "worthy men," he nevertheless pointed out that all of them were athletes—a coincidence that inflamed the otherwise baseless rumor that the Fleece was planning to consolidate itself with the Athletic Association. He argued that the selection of the three athletes did nothing to make the Fleece a "representative group" of outstanding students when the presidents of Phi Beta Kappa, the student body, and the senior class were not members, nor were the editors of the university's publications or its best debaters. He concluded by ruefully observing that the "Golden Fleece—like the old gray mare—ain't what she 'uster' be."[24]

The controversy was stoked further by a skirmish involving Carroll and Argonauts John Frazier Glenn Jr. and Addison Exum Warren, reported on the front page of the *Tar Heel* on December 9, 1926. According to the paper, when Carroll was attending his initiation into the Sigma Upsilon literary fraternity, he wore a placard on his back bearing the words "Pledged to the Golden Fleece." Glenn, construing the placard as an insult, snatched it from Carroll's back and handed it to Warren, who angrily tore it up. In the presence of "a crowd of awe stricken students," Warren and Carroll then engaged in an "impersonal argument" about whether the placard was intended as an insult or a joke and whether the Fleece "stood for reason or brawn."

Carroll's subsequent Driftwood Fire column was caustic. Announcing that "the fight for the slaughter of these gilded sheep [has] begun," he wrote, "If ever a wolf masqueraded in sheep's clothing, that wolf is Golden Fleece." He charged that just as the Fleece "depends for its existence upon the melodrama of its ceremony, mysticism, and voodooism," its members' conduct in the placard incident was "an appeal to emotions by kindergarten bug-a-boo tactics." Claiming that "the torn sign belonged to Sigma Upsilon," he then demanded the Fleece provide an "official explanation" for its members' assault against the fraternity.[25]

Carroll's campaign against the order did not go unchallenged. In the same day's "Open Forum" section of the *Tar Heel*, Robert Lee Dula, a non–Fleece member, called Carroll's attack on the order "a most puerile, unwarranted, and obnoxious attempt to cast slurs upon the reputation of the 'Highest Honorary Organization' on our campus." He defended the right of the order to choose those members it alone believed worthy of induction rather than to have its members chosen by a *Tar Heel* columnist. Characterizing the placard incident a few days later as a "childish attempt [by Carroll] to subject the Golden Fleece to the ridicule of the student body," he contended that "an apology should be due not from the Golden Fleece, but to the Golden Fleece and the student body."[26]

In January 1927, Carroll resumed his cause célèbre—this time through his membership in the Di. The day after the placard incident, Carroll had introduced a bill in the Di that the Senate "go on record as favoring the abolition of the Golden Fleece," but debate on the bill had been postponed until after the New Year.[27] At the time, the Di and its counterpart, the Phi, were no longer literary societies. In 1919, the Phi had been renamed the Philanthropic Assembly, and in 1925, the Di had changed its name to the Dialectic Senate. Neither organization had any campuswide student government powers, but they served as distinguished forums in which students formally debated the public and campus issues of their day.[28]

On the evening of January 18, 1927, the Di voted 11 to 9 in favor of Carroll's bill, albeit in modified form. Just before the debate began, Carroll had changed the wording of his bill to resolve "that the Di Senate go on record as *disapproving* the present organization known as Golden Fleece." The *Tar Heel* described the debate as "one of the best displays of the gentle arts of persuasion, of wit, and general parliamentary generalship that has been witnessed by the august walls of the senate in many a moon." Carroll and others in favor of the bill argued that the Fleece had failed to select members who were the "best in their chosen line . . . [and] University citizenship" and had also failed "to unify the campus socially and to kill dissension in politics." Those opposing the bill argued that these claims were factually without merit and contended that the Di had no right to interfere in the private affairs of the order. The Fleece members present at the debate chose to say nothing.[29]

The controversy did not end there. More than a year later, after Carroll had graduated, Lewis Taylor Bledsoe, who eventually became president of the Di Senate, resurrected Carroll's original bill to abolish the Fleece. Bledsoe's decision to revive an anti-Fleece movement was an about-face, as he was one of the senators who had spoken in defense of the order during the Di debate of 1927.[30] In the May 10, 1928, edition of the *Tar Heel*, Bledsoe wrote an open letter to the student body in which he contended that four of the eleven students inducted into the order that spring "did not rate the honor." He went on to complain that "not a single first-string football player" was chosen and that a "literary man" had not been selected for three years. He concluded by asserting that the Fleece had three options: it could select more qualified members, admit that "its standards are subject to human frailties and fraternity politics," or disband.[31]

As it turned out, many in the student body agreed with Bledsoe's complaints. On May 15, his bill was debated not only by the Di but also by the Phi in a joint session of the two societies. The bill, which was revised to read, "Resolved: that it is the opinion of the Di and Phi in joint session that the organization of Golden Fleece has become useless and should be abolished," carried by a three-to-one majority. After the vote, the Di and Phi sent a joint letter to the order informing it that they had "gone on record by an overwhelming majority as favoring the immediate abolition and disbanding of the Golden Fleece."[32]

After the Di-Phi vote, public opposition to the Fleece died out. The order did not respond to the letter and did not disband. Over the next four years, it continued to select approximately ten new Argonauts per year, and the *Tar Heel* continued to give front-page coverage to the annual tapping ceremony. By 1933, the order had clearly regained the standing it had enjoyed in the university community before 1926, as an April 1933 editorial in the *Daily Tar Heel* made clear: "The Golden Fleece is an independent order, free in the selection of its members from any sort of obligation. It chooses its members solely on their merits as leaders and men of character who have influenced constructively the University and its ideals. By no means are the dubious qualifications of office-holding a prerequisite to membership. For these reasons, it affords to each student the inspiration of its ideals and a goal which is the highest honor that can come as the culmination of a campus career."

This description of the order underscores a point about the order's purposes that was largely missed during the controversy of 1926–1928. Consistent with the order's early purpose, the Fleece typically sought to select members from all major walks of student endeavor. But particularly after 1913, the order's paramount constitutional mandate was to select *only* members who had "attained marked distinction" in one or more university endeavors and had otherwise shown themselves "to be of unimpeachable character [and] loyal to the University."[33] That is, the cardinal qualities of distinctive achievement, character, and loyalty to the university were not to be compromised by selecting members merely to represent each of the major student activities on campus. Thus, when in the fall of 1937 there were only three Argonauts on campus and they asked Professor Horace Williams whether they should conduct an immediate tapping to increase their numbers, Williams told them, "Take only the best." On the basis of that advice, the Argonauts waited to make their selections in the spring.[34]

Over time, the tendency of the order was to begin selecting more, not fewer, members each year and to increase the categories of persons eligible for membership. In 1904, the Constitution limited membership to juniors and seniors and specified that no more than eight juniors could be selected each year.[35] In May 1913, the Constitution was amended to permit the election of up to twelve new members per year, no more than ten of whom could be juniors and no more than three of whom could be graduate or professional students.[36] By 1981, the Constitution placed no limit on the number of new members who could be admitted. In practice, approximately eight new members were inducted each year from 1904 to 1940, sixteen per year from 1941 to 1970, and twenty-five to thirty-five per year from 1971 through 2004. After 1981, moreover, graduate or professional students were eligible for membership if they were in at least their second year of graduate work, with exceptions made for students in one-year graduate programs and for graduate or professional students who had received an undergraduate degree from the university. Tenured faculty, non-tenured faculty with at least five years of employment at the university at Chapel Hill, staff members with at least five years of employment at the university at Chapel Hill, and any other persons who "had made significant contributions to undergraduate student life" were eligible to become honorary members.[37] In the late 1970s, when the total student body exceeded 20,000, the order adopted a formal system for soliciting nominations of prospective members from the entire university community.[38]

Professor George Lensing, faculty advisor to the Fleece for the last quarter of its first century, summarized the evolution of the order's selection process: "As the University has grown and the total number of officially recognized student groups on campus has also grown, . . . I have noted the continuing attempt to identify for membership in the Fleece, not just leaders in student government or *The Daily Tar Heel,* or the Campus Y[MCA], but students who are contributing to the quality of life on this campus in significant ways from a wide variety of campus sources: all aspects of the arts, from the twenty-eight varsity athletic groups, from the twenty or more religious groups, and from students whose effectiveness and contributions come from more obscure corners of campus life." He explained the organization's consistency and fairness in selecting candidates for the annual tapping ceremony: "Spreading the net widely enough to identify worthy candidates for tapping remains a high priority, even as it has become more challenging. The process of selection is itself always difficult, arduous, sometimes frustrating, but also consistently thorough and careful. . . . I have also noted that the standard for selection remains extraordinarily high, and that is why the number of students and honoraries tapped throughout recent years remains relatively small in comparison with an ever-expanding student-body population.[39]

Women were first inducted into the order in 1972. At that time, they constituted approximately one-third of the student body. Before that change, the order's Constitution did not exclude women from membership, but none had been selected. In 1935, when women constituted 10 percent of the student body, they established a leadership society that was reorganized and named the Valkyries in 1941.[40] The Valkyries quickly became the most prestigious all-women's honor society on campus, and the Fleece occasionally met with the Valkyries to discuss campus issues such as the student honor system or fraternity-sorority problems.[41] In 1949, the Order of the Old Well was founded to recognize men and women for their humanitarian service to the university. Then, in 1957, the Society of Janus was established to recognize the contributions of men and women to the quality of residence hall life. Thus, by 1970, there were three honor societies on campus that recognized the achievements of women.

In the fall of 1971, the active order, believing that the Fleece could not continue to stand as the university's highest honorary society if women were not selected for membership, consulted with its alumni and with the Valkyries about admitting women into the order. After the Valkyries supported the proposal as one that would not compromise its identity as a distinctive women's honor society, the order consulted Deborah Ann Potter, a junior

Argonaut Deborah Ann Potter was consulted by the Fleece when they admitted the first women into the order. (Records of the Order of the Golden Fleece, University Archives, Louis Round Wilson Library, University of North Carolina at Chapel Hill)

who was an active member of the Association for Women Students, to help identify prospective women Argonauts.[42] In the spring of 1972, Potter and three other women—Mary Norris Preyer, Katherine Carlton McAdams, and Ann E. Queen—became the first females tapped into the order. In the 1980–1981 academic year, the Valkyries merged with the Order of the Grail (an all-male service honor society founded at the university in 1920) to form the Grail-Valkyries. By that time, the Fleece had selected over seventy women Argonauts over a period of ten years.

In its first one hundred years, the order has selected over 1,700 members. Just as these members have, in the words of the 1994 Constitution, exemplified "outstanding personal integrity, a superlative record of achievement, and service and loyalty to the University," they have also made significant contributions in many other walks of life. The roster of alumni includes an impressive array of individuals. The tables below illustrate the breadth of service and accomplishments of just some of the Fleece alumni.

Members' service and accomplishments exemplify a broader expectation envisioned by the founders of the Fleece. With the passing of the years, the Fleece has not only lived up to its constitutional purpose to recognize students "who meet the Order's highest standards," it has also established an aspiration for excellence and broader service that has become a core ideal of the order.[43]

MEMBERS' SERVICE & ACCOMPLISHMENTS

SERVICE TO THE UNIVERSITY

University Presidents

William D. Carmichael Jr.
(as acting president)
Harry Woodburn Chase
William Clyde Friday

Edward Kidder Graham
Frank Porter Graham
Gordon Gray
Clemmie Dixon Spangler Jr.

Chancellors*

William Brantley Aycock
Julius Levonne Chambers
(North Carolina Central University)
Robert Burton House
Christopher C. Fordham III
Paul Hardin

James R. Leutze (UNC-Wilmington)
William O. McCoy (as interim
chancellor)
J. Carlyle Sitterson
Nelson Ferebee Taylor

PUBLIC SERVICE

Governors of North Carolina

John Christoph Blucher Ehringhaus
Oliver Max Gardner
Luther Hartwell Hodges**

James Baxter Hunt Jr.
Terry Sanford
William Bradley Umstead

U.S. Congressmen

James Hayes Shofner Cooper
Alonzo Dillard Folger
Charles Raper Jonas
Allard Kenneth Lowenstein

L. Richardson Preyer
David Eugene Price
Terry Sanford
William Bradley Umstead

Members of the North Carolina House of Representatives

Arch Turner Allen Jr.
Philip Augustine Baddour Jr.
Marie Watters Colton†
James Gooden Exum Jr.
John Hosea Kerr Jr. (as speaker)
Kerr Craige Ramsay (as speaker)

Charles G. Rose Jr.
Wade Marvin Smith
Walter Frank Taylor (as speaker)
Jennifer Weiss
Willis P. Whichard
William H. Yarborough Jr.

(table continues)

*Chapel Hill campus unless otherwise noted.
**Hodges was also U.S. secretary of commerce under presidents John F. Kennedy and Lyndon B. Johnson.
†Colton was the first woman speaker pro tem of the House.

[47]

Members of the State Senate

Marc Basnight
Hargrove Bowles Jr.
Albert Lyman Cox (also
    Major General of the U.S. Army)
James Calvin Cunningham III
Archibald K. Davis

Joseph Colin Eagles Jr.
Howard Nathaniel Lee
Anthony Eden Rand
Ralph Henderson Scott
Richard Yates Stevens
Willis P. Whichard

Members of the Federal Judiciary

Jerry Richie Leonard (U.S. Bankruptcy judge)
James Bryan McMillan Sr. (U.S. District Court judge)
John Johnston Parker (chief judge, Fourth Circuit Court of Appeals)
J. Dickson Phillips Jr. (judge, Fourth Circuit Court of Appeals).

North Carolina Supreme Court Justices and Court of Appeals Judges

William Haywood Bobbitt (chief justice)
James Gooden Exum Jr. (chief justice)
Edward Greene (Court of Appeals)
Robert Carl Hunter (Court of Appeals)
Clifton Leonard Moore (associate justice)
Susie Marshall Sharp (chief justice)

Walter Parker Stacy (chief justice)
Willis Padgett Whichard (associate
    justice and Court of Appeals)
John Wallace Winborne (chief
    justice)

North Carolina Trial Court Judges

Craig Burdeen Brown (District Court)
Joe Moody Buckner (District Court)
Francis Osborne Clarkson (Superior Court)
Walter Edgar Crissman (Superior Court)
Mary Patricia De Vine (District Court)
Franklin Edward Freeman Jr. (Superior Court)
Hamilton Harris Hobgood (Superior Court)
Elbert Sidney Peele Jr. (Superior Court)
William Reid Thompson (Superior Court)

Other Notable Public Servants

Erskine Boyce Bowles, White House chief of staff to
    President William Jefferson Clinton
Roy Asberry Cooper III, North Carolina attorney general
Walter Estes Dellinger III, acting U.S. solicitor general
William Neil Thomas III, circuit court judge in Tennessee
Charles Walter Tillett, United Nations advocate and champion of "peace by law"

Newman Alexander Townsend, special assistant attorney general under
   President Franklin D. Roosevelt
Archibald Lee Manning Wiggins, under secretary of the U.S. Treasury

SERVICE IN THE FIELDS OF MEDICINE, SCIENCE, AND INVENTION

Medicine

Walter Reece Berryhill, founder of North Carolina's
   Area Health Education Centers program
Stuart Osborne Bondurant Jr., president of the Association of
   American Medical Colleges
George Lunsford Carrington, pioneer surgeon
Henry Toole Clark Jr., supervisor of Connecticut's health education
   and hospital system
James Evans Davis, president of the American Medical Association
Gordon H. DeFriese, president of the Association for Health Services Research
Hubert Benbury Haywood, president of the N.C. Medical Society
Thomas Grier Miller, president of the American College of Physicians
George F. Sheldon, president of numerous national surgery associations
Robert Wallace Wilkins, president of the American Heart Association

Science

Francis Collins, director of the National Genome Research Institute
Charles Holmes Herty Jr., pioneering metallurgist and chemical engineer
Howard Washington Odum, founder of the UNC-CH Institute for
   Research in Social Science

Invention

Frederick Phillips Brooks Jr., IBM computer developer
William Hermas Stephenson, developer of resuscitators and
   oxygen-breathing equipment

(table continues)

SERVICE IN BUSINESS, FINANCE, AND PHILANTHROPY

Business

Robert March Hanes, president of Wachovia Bank
Robert Obediah Huffman, president of Drexel Furniture
Paul Joseph Rizzo, executive vice-president of IBM
Archibald Lee Manning Wiggins, railroad executive

Finance

Thomas Callendine Boushall, banker
Archibald K. Davis, banker
Walter Royal Davis, financier
Luther Hartwell Hodges, banker
Richard Hampton Jenrette, financier

Nicholas Simon McPherson
  Johnston, financier
Frank Cresson Potts McGlinn Jr.,
  banker
Philip Woollcott, banker

Philanthropy

Agnew Hunter Bahnson, textile manufacturer and philanthropist
Eli N. Evans, Revson Foundation executive
Joel Lawrence Fleishman, Atlantic Foundation executive
George Alexander Heard, Ford Foundation executive
George Watts Hill Sr., banker and founder of Blue Cross Blue Shield
  of North Carolina
Thomas S. Kenan III, trustee of the William R. Kenan Jr. Charitable Trust
  and other philanthropic organizations
Thomas Willis Lambeth, Z. Smith Reynolds Foundation executive
Charles Edward Lovelace Jr., executive director of the John Motley Morehead
  Foundation
John Motley Morehead, head of Union Carbide and philanthropist
Mebane Moore Pritchett, executive director of the John Motley Morehead
  Foundation
Charles Galliard Tennent, Rotary International executive

SERVICE IN ARTS AND LETTERS

Music

Richard Adler, Broadway composer
James Kay Kyser, band leader
Thor Martin Johnson, director of the Cincinnati Symphony Orchestra
Benjamin Franklin Swalin, conductor of the N.C. Symphony Orchestra

Literature

Doris Waugh Betts, novelist
Franklin Taylor Branch, author
William Terry Couch, founding editor-in-Chief of *Collier's Encyclopedia*
Clement William Eaton, historian
Shelby Dade Foote, American Civil War historian
Paul Eliot Green, Pulitzer Prize–winning playwright
Harvey Hatcher Hughes, Pulitzer Prize–winning playwright
William Edward Leuchtenburg, historian and biographer of
    President Franklin D. Roosevelt
Armistead Jones Maupin Jr., author
Walker Percy, author
William Tannahill Polk, short story writer and journalist
Charles Phillips Russell, prolific writer of biographies
Thomas Clayton Wolfe, novelist and short story writer

Journalism

Donald Aaron Baer, media executive and White House communications
    director for President William Jefferson Clinton
John Grimes Branch, cartoonist
Orville Bentley Campbell, editor and publisher of the *Chapel Hill Weekly*
Walter Horace Carter, founder of the Pulitzer Prize–winning *Tabor City Tribune*
Joseph Lenoir Chambers, Pulitzer Prize–winning editor of the *Norfolk
    Virginia-Pilot*
Elbert Clifton Daniel Jr., executive editor of the *New York Times*
Jonathan Worth Daniels, editor of the *Raleigh News and Observer*
John Drescher, managing editor of the *Raleigh News and Observer*
Woody Lombardi Durham, sportscaster
Louis Harris, pollster
Allen Herbert Johnson III, managing editor of the *Winston-Salem Journal*
Jesse Weimar Jones, editor of the *Franklin Press* and president of
    the N.C. Press Association
Louis Kraar, Asian bureau chief of the *Wall Street Journal*
Charles Bishop Kuralt, CBS television reporter and program host
Alan Stewart Murray, *Wall Street Journal* bureau chief and NBC television
    news program host
Vermont Royster, Pulitzer Prize–winning editor of the *Wall Street Journal*
Donald Cleavenger Shoemaker, editor of the *Miami Herald*
William Davis Snider, editor of the *Greensboro Daily News*
Thomas Grey Wicker, bureau chief and columnist for the *New York Times*
Edwin Milton Yoder Jr., Pulitzer Prize–winning editorial writer and editor

(table continues)

A. Anson Dorrance IV, soccer coach, UNC-CH

Mia Hamm, women's Olympic and professional soccer player

Charles "Choo Choo" Justice, professional football player and football coach,
UNC-CH

Michael Jeffrey Jordan, professional basketball player

Frank J. McGuire, basketball coach, UNC-CH

Jane Bethel Preyer, women's professional tennis player

Dean E. Smith, basketball coach, UNC-CH

Susan Elizabeth Walsh, women's Olympic swimmer and inductee,
Verizon All-America Hall of Fame

Cindy Jo Werley, women's Olympic field hockey player

Elias Victor Seixas Jr., Wimbledon and U.S. Open tennis champion

CHAPTER FIVE

Tappings and Other Traditions

IN THE LATE EVENING of May 14, 1904, Claiborn McDowell Carr was solemnly escorted to the economics library on the third floor of the Alumni Building. There, in the presence of the eleven charter members of the order, all of whom wore robes, he became the first "neophyte" to be inducted into the Golden Fleece. Over the next two hours, at fifteen-minute intervals in an order predetermined by random lot, each of the seven other juniors who had been elected into the order was similarly inducted. When the ceremony ended just before midnight, the Fleece had formally established its class of active Argonauts for the 1904–1905 academic year.[1]

Beginning with the charter members, each new Argonaut was assigned a number corresponding with the order in which he was inducted. The first faculty advisors, Professors Horace Williams, Edward Kidder Graham, and Eben Alexander, were assigned the letters "A," "B," and "C," respectively. Each new member also received a pendant consisting of a small fleece cast in gold that was originally designed by Fred Mahler, a partner in H. Mahler Sons of Raleigh, North Carolina.[2] The reverse side of the ornament bore the Argonaut's number and the inscription "4/11/04," the date when Roach Stewart and Robert Herring convened the initial meeting of the student leaders at which the order was founded.[3] In later years, each new member was also given a certificate bearing the Argonaut's name, number, and, in Greek letters, the motto of the order: "Having dared to surpass the many, you sought the golden fleece."[4]

New members have always been selected by the active order, composed of those Argonauts who are enrolled as full-time students at the university.[5] Until 1922, the practice was to ask prospective members in advance whether they wanted to join the society and to notify them of their selection by letter.[6] Occasionally, the invitation was declined.[7] For the first ten years of the order, there was no public induction ceremony.

The first public "tapping" ceremony took place in the spring of 1914.[8] It resembled the reported 1915 tapping, which was held during the intermission of a satiric play put on by the senior class in Gerrard Hall: "At the intermission, hooded figures with white robes trimmed with gold entered the hall with their faces shrouded. They just moved through the hall, tapped the men, pinned on the ribbons [of white and gold], and left them to see the remainder of the play."[9] From 1916 to 1919, similar public tappings were held during the annual spring event of Junior or Senior Stunt Night.[10]

In the spring of 1920, the Fleece held its first independent public tapping, which in large part became the prototype of the present-day ceremony.[11] In that year, before a capacity crowd of students in Gerrard Hall, Argonaut Edwin Emerson White led off the event with a brief statement of the history and purpose of the order. University president Harry Woodburn Chase then introduced North Carolina governor Thomas Walter Bickett, who gave a short address in which he urged the audience to "clothe the future in bright dreams so that the years will make these dreams of today the facts of tomorrow."[12] The height of the ceremony that followed was described in the April 2, 1920, edition of the *Tar Heel* in a front-page article that was most likely written by then-editor (and later novelist) Thomas Wolfe, an Argonaut.[13] Wolfe wrote: "When the applause had finally subsided, and Governor Bickett had taken his seat, the Golden Fleece 'tappers' came in. . . . As the 'tapper' walked, now slowly, now rapidly, along the aisle, the silence became more marked. The 'tappers' would turn and go back toward the door only to return up the aisle. . . . No one knew whom the robed figures would tap. Indeed the robed figures themselves seemed equally undecided. Their Hamlet-like turning, this way and that, seemingly beset with indecision, was the impressive part which held the audience undecided whether or not to breathe for those intervals." Finally, the tappers, who were cloaked in black from head to toe and wore golden fleeces on their backs, chose the first neophyte, "and the silence gave way to applause." The remaining seven were chosen, and President Chase was tapped last. "The tapping was over," Wolfe concluded, "and the tappers retired, without ever having said a word."

The tapping ceremony included a featured speaker until 1936.[14] There was no keynote speaker from 1936 to 1954. During that period, however, the Fleece added other innovations to the ceremony that have carried forward to the present. By the late 1930s, for example, it included music and the reading of the Golden Fleece legend, which was originally adapted from *The Age of Fable* by Thomas Bulfinch and was later rendered in the form set out in the prologue to this history. In 1948, Jason William Henry Houston Miller befriended Carl Boettcher, a university employee who had carved decorative woodwork for churches in Europe and had fled Nazi Germany to start a new life in the United States. At Miller's request, Boettcher carved a large wooden Golden Fleece emblem that was first used in the 1949 tapping ceremony and is still used today.[15]

Argonaut William Robert Coulter described the 1949 ceremony in Memorial Hall—by that time complete with music, legend, and Fleece emblem: "As soon as the doors were locked, the hall was plunged into complete darkness, a gong shatters the gloom, and the organist begins the ceremony with solemn music." This was Wagner's "Entry of the Gods into Valhalla." Coulter's account continues: "Then the curtains are slowly drawn aside as a spotlight causes the Golden Fleece symbol to glow in the pitch-black silence. As the music fades, a voice resounds over the loudspeaker and gives the legend of the Golden Fleece. Again the music rises to a pitch and fades away as the Jason enters with a candle and gives his talk. As he slowly leaves the stage and disappears, the gong sounds and the tapping begins." At this point, "the two hooded giants of the Golden Fleece" enter "amid electrifying music"— more Wagner. The giants "stalk" the crowd, stop, and one taps the first Argonaut. Then, the giants begin stalking again, stop, the other taps an Argonaut, and they alternate until "the last man is tapped," at which point "the gong sounds." Coulter concluded: "As the stage lights come up slowly, the music . . . reaches a crescendo and the tappees file out upon the stage to be introduced by the Jason."[16]

In that year, William H. Miller gave the Jason's tapping address. His words to the audience about the new Argonauts would be quoted in many ceremonies thereafter:

Frank Weston Fenhagen being tapped in Memorial Hall in 1946 (Records of the Order of the Golden Fleece, University Archives, Louis Round Wilson Library, University of North Carolina at Chapel Hill)

Judge them for what they are as well as for what they have done for our University. The Fleece you see there is but the symbol of:

All the grueling hours of unselfish service;
Of courage in the face of scorn and adversity;
Of character and principle;
Of intellectual endeavor;
Of desire to give as well as receive of this University;
Of leadership in all the yearnings, ambitions, dreams, and visions of the heart;
Of the aspirations of the soul . . .

Now your journey is ended . . . You have dared to be above the average . . . You have lost yourself . . . and tonight in the darkness of this hall you will find the Golden Fleece.[17]

Beginning in the early 1950s and continuing to the present day, the tapping includes the reading of a citation for each new Argonaut that summarizes the achievements and contributions for which the member is being inducted. From time to time, some Argonauts have received the special honor of being retapped. U.S. Fourth Circuit Court of Appeals judge John Johnston Parker,[18] University of North Carolina president William Clyde Friday, and CBS News reporter Charles Bishop Kuralt were each tapped twice, while University of North Carolina president Frank Porter Graham was tapped on three separate occasions.

In 1955, the order resumed the practice of having a featured speaker at the tapping ceremony when William Haywood Bobbitt, then associate justice and later chief justice of the North Carolina Supreme Court, spoke at the event. This renewed practice was sporadic at first but became a regular tradition by the late 1960s. From 1980 onward, the keynote addresses became known as the "Frank Porter Graham Lectures on Excellence." Occasionally, the order reproduced a particular lecture in monograph form for distribution to its alumni.[19]

Immediately following the tapping ceremonies, the order has traditionally held a private banquet for the new Argonauts, the active order, and Fleece alumni.[20] The practice appears to have begun in 1930, although a spring banquet was held for active and alumni Argonauts as early as 1916.[21] At these banquets, usually held at the Carolina Inn,[22] "each Argonaut would rise, identify [himself or herself] by name, class and number, and proceed to say whatever was on [the member's] mind. These occasions were a rich mixture of nostalgia from the older Argonauts and the excited enthusiasm of the newly tapped members."[23] At times, alumni who were unable to attend would send letters with brief remarks of personal news or inspiration, which were read by the Jason or another attending member. In some years, the order had a featured banquet speaker in lieu of or in addition to a keynote speaker at the tapping ceremony. These banquet addresses were frequently as carefully prepared and eloquent as the tapping speeches. In addition to the post-tapping banquets, in 1939 the Fleece began the tradition of holding a breakfast for active and alumni Argonauts on commencement weekend.[24] Like the banquets, these breakfasts provided the members with an opportunity to renew friendships, meet new Argonauts, and make individual remarks.[25]

Throughout the history of the Fleece, the active order has kept in regular contact with the order's alumni. Although the alumni have no constitutional role or formal powers,[26] they are regularly advised about Fleece affairs and are frequently consulted about major initiatives undertaken by the active order. In addition, since 1949, the order has periodically published a complete roster of the Fleece alumni—commonly referred to as "the Blue Book"—which contains each member's Argonaut number, year of induction, and current address.[27] From the mid-1990s forward, the Blue Book has been updated every five years and is reproduced on the Golden Fleece website, which was established in 2002.[28]

The first formal alumni gathering took place at a banquet on November 14, 1905, and was reported in the November 23 edition of the *Tar Heel*. A similar reunion was held in the spring of 1923.[29] By the early 1970s, the Fleece had begun to hold a fall banquet for alumni Argonauts and their guests,[30] and in 1981 the Constitution prescribed that, in addition to the tapping banquet and commencement breakfast, there be "an annual banquet preceding each Homecoming."[31] In 1982, the order turned this banquet into a more informal wine-and-cheese reception held during homecoming weekend or on some other fall weekend. The tradition continues to this day.

Until the early 1980s, the active order was constantly compelled to solicit funds from its alumni to defray the costs of annual Fleece events and other operating expenses, such as mailings, the Golden Fleece page in the *Yackety Yack*, the publication of the Blue Book, and the publication of citations for new Argonauts in the *Daily Tar Heel*. For over eighty years, new members were assessed dues, but that source of funds was rarely sufficient to cover the order's annual expenses.[32] In 1946, the financial situation became so desperate that the active order even sought passage of a bill in the student legislature to pay for the Fleece's *Yackety Yack* page. Quite appropriately, this proposal was "thunderously defeated [as the inappropriate] use of public monies for the benefit of a private group."[33]

In 1947, the order first entertained the idea of establishing a trust fund that would provide a regular source of income to cover basic operating expenses.[34] In the early 1950s, an anonymous donor established a small trust that provided modest interest payments to the order. In 1983, under the leadership of Argonauts James Clarence Wallace, John Lassiter Sanders, and Thomas Eugene Terrell Jr., the Fleece alumni established the Golden Fleece Foundation.[35] This is a nonprofit charitable corporation with an endowment whose earnings meet the annual operating expenses of the order and obviate the need for assessing dues from new Argonauts and soliciting contributions from the alumni. The initial funding goal for the endowment was reached in the early 1990s, and since that time the fund has steadily grown under the management of the university's investment office.[36]

The organizational stability of the order was further enhanced in 1983 when Jason Robert Edward Johnson wrote the first Jason's Handbook.[37] To be kept in two loose-leaf binders, one for the current Jason and one in the Fleece archives, it set out the duties of the officers of the order together with detailed information about Fleece tappings, other traditions, and the duties of the active order.[38] Johnson's Jason's Handbook has been maintained and updated.

In a further effort to help ensure that the Fleece maintain a permanent record of activities, in the fall of 2003 the active order adopted an amendment to the Fleece By-Laws to mandate that the incumbent Jason, with the assistance of the grammateus and the Chrystopher, compile "complete and detailed records of all meetings, deliberations, activities, correspondence, financial reports, public and private events and lectures, citations for new members, and the names of the officers of the Order."[39] The amendment mandated that each year's Jason was responsible for transmitting a copy of these records to the order's archives.[40] In this way, the Fleece formally codified its intent to preserve the order's tappings and other traditions for future generations of Argonauts.

CHAPTER SIX

Promoting Unity and Student Responsibility

THE FIRST CLASS OF ARGONAUTS returned to Chapel Hill for the 1904–1905 academic year determined to address the central problem on campus that had led to the founding of the order: "to restore unity to college life." With deep divisions between the frats and non-frats, pervasive hazing of first-year students, and no campuswide structure of student self-government, the university was, in Professor Williams's words, fractured by "friction and harshness—oftentimes ugliness in student life."[1]

That ugliness became evident in November 1904 when the first-year medical class alleged that some members of the undergraduate sophomore class had "insulted" a first-year medical student. The precise nature of the insult is unknown. Although the offending students offered to apologize, the medical students voted 37 to 11 to demand that the Faculty Executive Committee (which was then charged with responsibility for all matters of student discipline) expel the offending sophomores from the university. Realizing that the matter could not be dealt with informally, the sophomore class asked the Fleece to help resolve the controversy.[2]

The order immediately seized upon this request as an opportunity to eradicate the perennial problem of hazing. At the suggestion of Professor Williams, it decided to have Jason Claiborn McDowell Carr and two other Argonauts appear publicly before the Faculty Executive Committee to propose "that the [offending] members of the sophomore class be allowed to remain in the University on condition that the sophomore class use its influence to keep hazing out of the University."[3] The committee readily accepted this proposal, which had been agreed to by the sophomore class, and dismissed all disciplinary charges against the offending students. In recounting how the controversy was resolved, the November 16, 1904, edition of the *Tar Heel* noted that "the order does not intend to act as arbitrator in college affairs but took the action it did in this case simply to avert what might have been a great division in University life, and also to induce the Sophomores to abolish hazing."[4]

The same edition of the *Tar Heel* carried an editorial written by Argonaut Frank McLean, the paper's editor-in-chief. McLean opined that the "excitement" over the sophomores' dispute would mean "the end of hazing in the University," which only a class of sophomores "early in the year" could bring about. McLean went on to explain that hazing had seemed to disappear in the past only to be revived due to the actions of freshmen who, when they "ceased to feel the influence of overpowering physical force," also "forgot that there are natural distinctions between men who have grown into University life and men who know nothing about it." He concluded: "When a Freshman forgets this there is an almost inevitable reminder coming for him. Freshmen, remember that you are FRESHMEN."[5]

The so-called Soph-Med Affair was the first and last time that the Fleece would allow its position on an issue affecting the welfare of the university to be made public in the order's name. From that time forward, as prescribed by the order's Constitution, all works of the Fleece were conducted privately, behind the scenes, and never in the name of the order.[6] As Argonaut William Robert Coulter explained years later, "The work of the group was to remain anonymous, with the specific actions effected by members as individuals who could best fight for the Fleece ideals without bringing censure upon the group over differences of opinion."[7]

Consistent with this behind-the-scenes approach, within a few weeks after the Fleece interceded in the Soph-Med Affair, the order quietly implemented two follow-up initiatives that were intended to address future incidents of hazing. The first of these was designed to give effect to McLean's editorial quoted above. On November 19, 1904, the Fleece secretly posted the following notice in a number of conspicuous places on campus:

FRESHMEN!
READ, MARK, DIGEST.
    1. Show respect to upper classmen.
    2. Bear in mind the difference between an honored "Senior" at a prep school and a freshman at the University.
    3. Beware of monopolizing the Post office and drug stores.
BE SEEN AND NOT HEARD[8]

Four days later, the *Tar Heel* reported that "nobody claims the honor of putting up the posters but the general opinion is that the Sophomores are responsible." The paper went on to announce that, in light of the posters, the senior and junior classes had passed resolutions supporting the sophomores' attempts to keep the freshmen "in their places."

The order's second follow-up initiative was the boldest and

most far-reaching. The experience of the Soph-Med Affair had underscored the need for a regular forum through which students could mediate class controversies and other issues of student discord. In addition, the order recognized that purely voluntary pledges or resolutions by the classes to address campuswide problems, such as hazing or other forms of divisiveness in student life, would be short-lived in the absence of a formal, student-run structure to enforce those commitments. At bottom, the Argonauts believed that to restore true unity to college life, the students themselves would have to take formal responsibility for their affairs.

There was, however, no real precedent for student self-government. Before 1904, various efforts to establish a viable form of student government had been largely ineffectual. For many years, the Dialectic and Philanthropic literary societies had loosely assumed the responsibility of investigating and taking action in cases of cheating and other forms of student misconduct. But the societies, being naturally protective of their members, were often loathe to tattle on their own, and there was no peer group to discipline students who were not members of one of the societies. Efforts by the individual classes to form committees to investigate and discipline offending students had been similarly ineffective.[9] As a result, the primary responsibility and power over all matters of student behavior and discipline continued to be held by the faculty.[10]

To change this system to one of student self-rule, on November 13, 1904, the order met privately with President Francis Venable to propose the establishment of a seven-member University Council consisting of the presidents of the three upper classes, a second-year student from each of the professional schools to be elected by the entire school, and a representative of the senior class to be elected by the other six. The senior elected by the six other members would preside over the council but would not be entitled to vote except in the case of a tie. The purpose of the council would be to dispose of all cases of hazing and violations of the honor system and to arbitrate class differences.[11]

In late November 1904, President Venable called a meeting of the class presidents to propose the structure and function of this new council. He did not reveal the source of the idea. Each of the class presidents then called a meeting of his class, and all of the classes endorsed the proposal. By the end of the week, the University Council had been established as the first formal instrument of student self-government at the university.[12] The 1908–1909 *Student Handbook* described it as "the concrete expression of the moral University." It explained the council's purpose as follows: "The Council is not an organization of policemen, nor is it based upon a system of espionage. When any student is felt by his fellow students to be unworthy to remain in the University, the Council takes cognizance of this feeling. It examines into the matter, finds the facts in the case, and decides upon the justice of that feeling. If the student is found guilty of conduct unworthy of a University man, he is requested by the Council to leave the University. . . . The student sentiment expresses itself in this way not only in cases of so flagrant a violation of the honor system as cheating, but also in cases of continued drunkenness, gambling, and such other forms of misconduct."[13]

The success of these early efforts to restore unity to university life were soon tested. In the fall of 1905, the Fleece called upon the upper classes to renew their pledges of the previous year to ban hazing if the freshman class would agree to abide by certain rules of behavior and decorum.[14] Jason Agnew Hunter Bahnson and Argonaut Thomas Grier Miller met privately with leaders of the senior and junior classes to propose that a joint committee of the upper classes come up with a uniform set of rules that might be imposed upon the freshmen.[15] The committee was established but ultimately failed to agree upon rules that were acceptable to all.[16] Nevertheless, both classes adopted resolutions to report any incidents of hazing to the University Council for appropriate action.[17]

The viability of the new University Council was soon tested— three times. The first test came in 1910 after the council suspended a student for stealing. The student appealed to the Faculty Executive Committee, which reversed the decision and reinstated the student, apparently on the strength of representations by a local minister, who vouched for the student's good character. In protest, the council resigned as a body. The students held mass meetings demanding their right to unfettered self-government, and the *Tar Heel* criticized the faculty's action in several sharply worded editorials. The matter was ultimately resolved in a compromise by which the council was designated the primary body with the power to deal with issues of student behavior but the Faculty Executive Committee, which would now consist of three faculty members chosen by the council, was established to hear cases on appeal. Under the new arrangement, the council was renamed the "Student Council."[18]

The second test occurred when the campus was rocked by a hazing incident that ended in tragedy. In the early morning hours of September 13, 1912, Isaac William Rand, a freshman, was being hazed by a group of sophomores. He fell from the top of a barrel, cut his jugular vein on a broken bottle, and bled to death. Under pressure from the governor and the state press, President Venable

appointed a special faculty committee to conduct a full investigation, which resulted in the dismissal of the sophomores responsible and further disciplinary action against eighteen other students
who had been involved in several unrelated hazing incidents. The
Student Council was bypassed altogether.[19] This incident made it
clear to students "that student governing powers could be forfeit-
ed by student government officers not understanding their re-
sponsibilities, [and] it awakened them to the necessity of vigorous
and sustained action in the effort to retain their liberties."[20]

The third test came during a renewed outbreak of hazing one
night in the early fall of 1917. A group of upperclassmen went on
a rampage from one dormitory to another, ransacking freshmen's
rooms and provoking fights. As the fracas escalated, Argonaut
William Marvin York, who was president of the senior class and
chairman of the Student Council, tried to intervene by stepping
into the crowd and pleading with the rioters to stop. When they
refused and pushed him aside, he began writing down the names
of the hazers in the open, where all could see what he was doing.
When that did not stop them, he followed them from one dormitory to another, continuing to record the names and actions of the
offending students.[21]

At midnight, he called a special meeting of the Student Council, gave a full report of what he had seen, and reported the
names of the hazers. They were later afforded a hearing and suspended from the university for the rest of the semester. Shortly af-
terward, university president and Argonaut Edward Kidder Graham praised the actions of the council and its chairman in an
address to the entire student body. At long last, the Student Council had come into its own as an effective, enduring, and unifying
force in the life of the university.[22]

By the close of 1917, the unity the Fleece had sought to restore to student life for over a decade had finally been realized. Hazing was under control, the old divisions between the classes and the frats and non-frats had given way to a more considerate student spirit, and the students had successfully taken responsibility for their own affairs by establishing a viable and durable structure of self-government. The *Tar Heel* proclaimed that "a noticeable elevation of student sentiment" had occurred in the previous five years, citing remarks made by the dean in his report to the university's president and by President Graham himself in his report to the university's Board of Trustees. The *Tar Heel* credited "the Honor spirit in student government" with responsibility for the change and maintained that the change itself had "been one of the chief factors in strengthening the University in the state."[23]

The order continued its efforts to preserve this unified spirit in the years after 1917. In the fall of 1931, for example, members of the Fleece met with Duke's student body president and the chairman of the Duke Honor Society to come up with a plan to help "unify the feeling" between Carolina and Duke in the face of their heated football rivalry. Because of this collaboration, just before the game started that year, the bands from both universities marched onto the field together, and the captains of each team gave a short talk about sportsmanship and good will.[24] In 1948, when the campus was still fragmented in the aftermath of World War II, the order organized an orientation program for incoming freshmen and sponsored a leadership conference for the heads of all of the fraternities.[25] In the 1952–1953 academic year, when a rash of panty raids erupted on campus, the Fleece worked with administration officials to help ensure that the raids did not escalate into uncontrolled mob violence.[26]

Occasionally, the order was involved in unifying initiatives of a more political nature. In November 1957, for example, Jason Thomas Willis Lambeth, Argonaut George Robinson Ragsdale, and other members of the order quietly helped to organize a re-call of the incumbent editor of the *Daily Tar Heel*, Neil Bass.[27] Bass had developed a reputation as an instigator of unwarranted divisiveness in the university community for what many believed were his "irresponsible" attacks on the Student Health Service's efforts to deal with a campuswide epidemic of the Asian flu and on the administration's support of the right of the head football coach to discipline his players for violating team training rules. In addition, many students believed that Bass had shirked his re-sponsibilities as a student leader by refusing to participate in the chancellor's administrative planning conferences when he was the first *Daily Tar Heel* editor to be invited to those high-level meetings.[28] In the end, Bass was soundly defeated in the recall election and replaced by a new editor, Doug Eisele, a non–Fleece member whose candidacy was supported by the order.

Another political issue that divided the campus came to a head in the mid-1970s. As early as 1955, students, faculty members, and administrators had complained about the efficacy of the campus Honor Code, particularly its so-called rat clause, which made it an offense for a student to fail to "report any violation of the Code of which he or she [had] knowledge." Efforts to reform the code, which began in 1969, culminated in the adoption of the 1974 In-strument of Student Judicial Governance, but it retained the rat clause as part of the Honor Code.[29] As mounting criticism of the code threatened to spawn a movement for wholesale repeal of the honor system, in the 1975–1976 academic year the Fleece, under the leadership of Jason Charles Thomas Humphries, conducted a comprehensive survey of student and faculty concerns about the new Instrument of Student Judicial Governance.[30] Based in large part on the results of that survey, in 1978 the instrument and the code were amended to delete the rat clause and to increase the severity of penalties for academic cheating.[31]

These projects were the product of regular discussions at Fleece meetings about ways to bind together and better the university community as a whole. The early constitutions of 1904 and 1913 mandated that the members come to each meeting prepared to discuss one or more specific topics, and the later constitutions of 1981 and 1994 prescribed that the order hold at least one meeting per month.[32] Some of the topics discussed over the years included the purpose of the university, the adequacy of state budget appropriations for the campus, ways to beautify the campus, how to control violence during student protests of the Vietnam War, the need to increase student financial aid, improving the Office of Student Affairs, the use of student activities fees, enhancing the administration of the Student Health Service, ways to ease campus parking and transportation problems, the need for better communication between the administration and student leaders, the selection criteria for choosing a new chancellor, and controlling tuition increases.[33]

But formal projects undertaken by Fleece members as a group were relatively rare. For the most part, the modus operandi of the order was to treat campus problems discussed at Fleece meetings by encouraging each member to address those problems in individual ways, usually through the efforts of members to exert influence in the particular branches of university life in which they participated. In addition, in many years, private meetings of the order were held with the president of the university, the chancellor, other administrators, leaders of the faculty, and leaders of various student organizations, including other campus honor societies. In this way, the order sought to serve as a source of quiet counsel and support to those in leadership positions throughout the university and to share ideas about ways in which to enhance the overall welfare of the community.

In all of these cases over the years, whether the efforts of the Fleece were undertaken as group projects or through the individual efforts of its members, the overriding theme remained the same—to promote a spirit of wholesome unity within the campus community. In keeping with the core philosophy of the founding members, that unity was sought through endeavors that emphasized accountability over irresponsibility, concord over discord, and oneness over division.

CHAPTER SEVEN

Frank Porter Graham
Argonaut of the Half-Century

WHEN THE NATIONAL ASSOCIATION of State Universities
and Land Grant Colleges celebrated its centennial in 1987, it
asked each member institution to name up to ten distinguished
alumni from its ranks. They were to be "individuals of outstanding character and a credit to their professions and communities."
From all the nominees, the association's Centennial Committee
was to select a smaller group of "Centennial Alumni." Chancellor
and Argonaut Christopher C. Fordham III asked the university's
Alumni Association board to send him suggestions for nominations from the Chapel Hill campus. The board recommended that
he make only one nomination: Frank Porter Graham. He did so.
From more than 1,200 nominees, the Centennial Committee selected 125 Centennial Alumni, including Graham.[1] He was awarded this distinction almost four decades after he stepped down
from the presidency of the university in 1949 and some fifteen
years after his death in 1972.

Given Graham's enduring stature in the university community,
it should come as no surprise that at the annual tapping ceremony

on April 27, 1953, the Fleece selected him as its "Argonaut of the Half-Century." Three months earlier, the active order had solicited nominations for the honor from its alumni in planning for the order's fiftieth anniversary observance (which, as we now know, should have taken place a year later). The nomination request was for "the member, now living, who best exemplifies the ideals of the Golden Fleece in his life, in the example he has set for others, and in the contributions he has made to the University, the State, the nation and to mankind." Out of seventeen nominations submitted by the alumni, Graham received the majority of votes on the first ballot.[2]

Jason Julian Dewey Mason Jr. announced Graham's selection for the honor on the evening of April 27 before a packed crowd in Memorial Hall. As Graham's citation for the award, Mason read to the audience the nomination sent him on March 6, 1953, by Argonaut Douglass Hunt, then a lawyer in Washington, D.C.[3] The nomination began: "Ordinarily I think it a sterile exercise, at best, to select a 'man of the week' or of the year or even of the half-century. But there are times when the choice is so clear and the merit of a single person so shining that all his fellows gladly acknowledge his worth and take comfort from his presence among them. . . . No man has outdone [Graham] in service to the Fleece, to the University, to the State of North Carolina, to the United States, and now—may his patience prevail—to the peace-seeking peoples of the world." Hunt went on to laud Graham for displaying "the Christian grace of charity." "The words that describe him," he explained, "are the short words that are the only ones that really matter: he is kind, he has been sad at times; and he has known grief; he smiles a lot; he has grit; he has faith; more than anyone I have ever met he loves mankind—even those men who

Frank Porter Graham, Argonaut of the Half-Century (North Carolina Collection, Louis Round Wilson Library, University of North Carolina at Chapel Hill)

have despitefully used him; he is good; he does his duty first; he has a free mind; and he loves liberty for others as for himself. He is the measure of what men will be in that day when mankind, though not perfected, are sufficiently improved to be tolerable to themselves and to each other."[4]

Graham's long service to the university began when he was an undergraduate at Carolina from 1905 to 1909. He was class president, president of the honor council and of the YMCA, editor of the *Tar Heel*, and active in baseball and cheerleading. He was tapped into the order in 1908 and elected Jason. In the spring of 1909, his Senior Class Day speech urging greater state support for the university so impressed President Francis Venable that he had it printed and distributed throughout the state.

After finishing law school at Chapel Hill in 1913, Graham began his career with the university as secretary of the campus YMCA. One year later, when his cousin, Argonaut Edward Kidder Graham, became president, "Dr. Frank"—as his students later affectionately called him—taught a course in American history. Invigorated by the classroom and intent on making teaching a career, in 1915 he entered Columbia University, where he earned a master's degree the following year.

His postgraduate education was interrupted by the First World War, during which he served stateside in the marines. When the war ended, he returned to Chapel Hill as dean of students, resumed teaching courses in history, and led a successful public campaign to increase state appropriations for the university. From 1921 to 1924, he continued his postgraduate studies at the University of Chicago, the Brookings Institution in Washington, D.C., and the London School of Economics. Returning to the classroom in Chapel Hill in 1925, he became an active speaker and advocate of causes such as establishing community libraries throughout the state, workers' compensation, and a bill of rights for labor. Five years later, with the support of North Carolina governor and Argonaut Oliver Max Gardner, Graham became president of the university.

During his tenure as president from 1930 to 1949, Graham was a zealous champion of academic freedom and a staunch defender of the university as a free voice of intellectual, political, and social expression. During the Great Depression, when the state's depleted treasury forced drastic budget cuts, he averted disaster for the university by hitting the road to garner financial support from private sources throughout the state.

After Franklin D. Roosevelt became president of the United States in 1933, he drew Graham away from the campus to serve on numerous national boards and commissions, including the National War Labor Board, the National Defense Mediation Board, the Oak Ridge Institute of Nuclear Studies board, the Commission on Education, and the Commission on Civil Rights. In 1947, U.S. secretary of state George Marshall asked Graham to serve on a United Nations committee to negotiate a dispute between the colonial Dutch powers and the Indonesian forces that were establishing an independent republic. During these years, Graham handled much of the university's business by telephone and on weekends, and on Sunday evenings he often invited students to an open house at his residence, where they discussed whatever issues were on their minds.[5]

Shortly after Graham returned to Chapel Hill in 1949, North Carolina governor W. Kerr Scott, at the urging of many prominent Democrats (including Argonaut Jonathan Worth Daniels, who was editor of the *News and Observer* in Raleigh), appointed Graham to the U.S. Senate to fill the vacancy caused by the death of Senator J. Melville Broughton. A year later, Graham was defeated in the senatorial primary that would have enabled him to serve out the balance of Broughton's term. The unexpected loss was largely the result of a bitter campaign in which conservative political forces made Graham's liberal views on race and civil liberties major issues in the primary.

But Graham's national service did not end upon his leaving the Senate in 1950. In January 1951, at the request of President Harry S. Truman, Graham chaired a labor management conference to help settle labor disputes during the Korean War. Later, he was called upon once more to serve on a United Nations commission, this time to forge a resolution to the long-standing dispute between India and Pakistan over Kashmir. In 1967, he left the United Nations and retired to Chapel Hill, where he remained until his death in 1972.[6]

In his own words, Graham believed in a world "where democracy is without vulgarity, excellence is without arrogance; where the answer to error is not terror and the response to a difference in color, race, religion, and ideas . . . is not discrimination, exploitation, or intimidation; where and when men are free, the way of progress is not subversion, the respect for the past is not reaction, and the hope of the future is not revolution; where the majority is without tyranny, the minority is without fear, and all people have hope."[7]

Seventeen years after Graham's death, at the order's tapping banquet on the evening of April 7, 1989, Argonaut and chancellor emeritus of Vanderbilt University George Alexander Heard called Graham "an enormously appealing man who knew more people and had more friends than any other person in North Carolina."

In his career, Heard recalled, Graham had "relished the stimulation and satisfaction of lobbying, of negotiating and arguing and pleading, of working the corridors in the interests of his main mission and first love, the University at Chapel Hill." Heard continued:

> By training, Dr. Frank knew, in Sir John Seeley's words, that "History is past politics, and politics present history." By temperament and instinct, he loved the good fight for the good cause, the contest that gave his extraordinary personal qualities a full field to play upon. . . . He was pervasively a person of moral values; he was also equally a man of action. . . . He was a marvelous politician. He was a politician in the fundamental sense, like Washington and Lincoln and Gandhi, who recognizes that little predictable good in human association emerges from accident, who recognizes the greatest good will comes from purposeful energies welded with skill to high purposes. . . . His leadership was his personality. . . . He was the most magnanimous, virtuous, and consequential person many of us would ever come to know.[8]

Frank Graham exemplified the best of the Fleece's ideals, serving the university to bind its diverse forces together and to harmonize its mission, as best he could at the time, with the people of the state. Most notably, he did so with a strength of personal character and conviction that did not bow to petty political agendas. As a man of intense faith, he believed in the equality of all persons endowed with the fundamental rights of life, liberty, and property. He thought the university should educate its students about those rights and act as their champion, not only for the benefit of the state but for the whole of the nation.

CHAPTER EIGHT

The Speaker Ban Law Controversy

BEGINNING WITH FRANK PORTER GRAHAM'S presidency of the Consolidated University of North Carolina—which the North Carolina General Assembly established in 1931 by joining North Carolina State College at Raleigh and the North Carolina College for Women at Greensboro with the original campus at Chapel Hill—the university gradually became a center of intellectual and social activism that began to outpace changes in the state's social and political environment. This trend continued under the presidencies of Argonaut Gordon Gray (1950–1955) and Argonaut William Clyde Friday (1956–1986).

In those years, the university enjoyed the support of a one-hundred-member Board of Trustees (one member from each county in the state) and a smaller trustee Executive Committee that were generally successful in maintaining public support for the institution and preventing unwarranted political intrusion into university affairs. But this institutional freedom was abruptly compromised in the summer of 1963 in what became known as the "Speaker Ban Law controversy." For the next four years,

Fleece members within and outside the university would join other defenders of academic freedom in a struggle to preserve the university as a free and progressive force in the life of the state, region, and nation.

The Speaker Ban Law, formally titled "House Bill 1395: An Act to Regulate Visiting Speakers at State Supported Colleges and Universities," was enacted by the General Assembly on the afternoon of June 25, 1963, the last day of the year's legislative session. In a rare suspension of House and Senate rules, the bill was rammed through both legislative chambers in a little over an hour. There was no public hearing and no opportunity for opponents to speak.[1] The law was a clear affront to the First Amendment's freedom-of-speech guarantee and the Fourteenth Amendment's due process prohibition of vague statutes.[2] It denied speaking privileges on state-supported campuses to "any person" who was "a known member of the Communist Party" or was "known to advocate the overthrow of the Constitution of the United States or the State of North Carolina" or had "pleaded the Fifth Amendment of the Constitution of the United States in refusing to answer any question with respect to Communist or subversive connections or activities."[3]

When President Friday learned of the impending enactment of the bill on the afternoon of June 25 from fellow Fleece member and chancellor of the Chapel Hill campus William Brantley Aycock, he and Frederick Henry Weaver, then secretary of the consolidated university and also an Argonaut, hastened to the legislative building in Raleigh to try to stop the passage of the measure. They were too late. By the time they arrived, the bill had already been sent to the enrolling office, and the legislature had adjourned. Friday told reporters he would "do everything possible" to oppose the law, which he politely characterized as "totally un-necessary."[4]

On a superficial level, the Speaker Ban Act appeared to be an extension of the anticommunist fever that had originated with the McCarthyism of the 1950s and culminated in the Cuban Missile Crisis of October 1962 at the height of the Cold War between the United States and the Soviet Union. Many members of the General Assembly were irked by the alleged "leftist radicalism" of some students on the Chapel Hill campus who, through fledgling organizations such as the Student Peace Union, the New Left Club, and the Progressive Labor Club, opposed U.S. anticommunist aid to South Vietnam, sponsored occasional discussion groups on Marxism and problems of Third World development, and espoused various socialistic and anticapitalist agendas. By October 1962, the perception that the campus had turned into a "Red nest" led to the adoption of a resolution by the Chapel Hill affiliate of the American Legion calling for a formal legislative investigation "to determine to what extent, if any, Marxism ha[d] permeated the University." Thus, one of the sponsors of the Speaker Ban Bill described its purpose as being to "prevent card-carrying Communists from using the Campus of the University as a forum."[5]

But below the surface, the driving issue behind the Speaker Ban Law was not Reds, but race.[6] By the spring of 1963, the Jim Crow system had entered its terminal phase. White supremacy (rarely so called in North Carolina) had served as the long-standing platform for the political power of many North Carolinians. In May and early June 1963, civil rights demonstrations that largely paralleled the movement of nonviolent civil disobedience spearheaded by Martin Luther King Jr. in Birmingham, Alabama, had sprung up in Greensboro, Durham, Chapel Hill, Winston-

Salem, Charlotte, and other North Carolina cities. In Raleigh, Argonaut Allard Kenneth Lowenstein, then on the political science faculty at North Carolina State College and an antisegregation activist, took Angie Brooks, the Liberian ambassador to the United States, to the whites-only coffee shop at the Sir Walter Hotel and to the S&W Cafeteria. Both establishments refused to serve her. Lowenstein thereafter helped organize a series of civil rights demonstrations and sit-ins by students, faculty members, and African Americans in the heart of the downtown capitol district. On May 8, 1963, ninety-two blacks were arrested when they demonstrated at the Sir Walter Hotel and the S&W Cafeteria. A month later, another round of arrests occurred when blacks arrived with their suitcases to register at the Sir Walter in what came to be known as the "suitcase sit-ins." As a result of these protests and protests elsewhere, by mid-June 1963 a number of cities in the North Carolina Piedmont had begun to take steps to desegregate their hotels, restaurants, theaters, and other places of public accommodation.[7]

The charge that Communism was behind these demonstrations stemmed largely from the twisted logic of racism. Because "Negroes" were inferior, unskilled, and uneducated—so the thinking went—they could not possibly be competent to launch a coordinated and systematic challenge to segregation on their own. By this logic, white students and white faculty members such as Lowenstein were the true leaders of the insurrection against segregation, and their behavior could only be explained if they were believers in Communist ideology, which included the tenet that racial integration was essential to "social equality."[8] What peeved many legislators the most was watching these university whites standing and sitting shoulder to shoulder with blacks at the Sir

Walter Hotel, where out-of-town members of the General Assembly usually resided during the legislative session.[9]

In reality, the university was hardly a hotbed of Communism. Lowenstein abhorred Communism, as did President Friday and Chancellor Aycock. There were no Communist faculty members at any of the UNC campuses, and from the late 1940s to the early 1960s students and administrators often excluded Communists from speaking on university campuses. In October 1962, Chancellor Aycock issued a statement to the Associated Press that he "had no evidence of any Communist cell on campus, or any Communist student in the University." Moreover, the notion that the university community was aiding and abetting the eradication of racial segregation under the influence of Communism was belied by the fact that many students staunchly opposed Communism, were largely indifferent to the civil rights movement, and shunned radicalism.[10]

The primary target of the Speaker Ban Law was the campus at Chapel Hill. Over time, many in the General Assembly had grown impatient with the flagship institution's alleged liberalism. In the 1920s, president of the university and Fleece member Harry Woodburn Chase upheld the university's freedom to teach and publish science by successfully joining the resistance to the legislature's efforts to enact the Poole Bill, which sought to prohibit the teaching of evolution.[11] In the 1930s and 1940s, when Argonaut Frank Porter Graham was president, he drew the ire of many in the conservative political establishment by publishing an "Industrial Bill of Rights" that advocated the extension of substantive due process, equal protection, and First Amendment rights to all persons "without regard to birthplace, race, ownership or labor status, unionism or non-unionism, religion, politics, or economic views." He refused to prohibit a black man, Langston Hughes, from speaking on the Chapel Hill campus, declined demands that he fire a professor for dining with a black man who was reputed to be a Communist, and publicly rebuffed another legislative call to enact the antievolution Poole Bill.[12] As mentioned in chapter 7, after being appointed by North Carolina governor W. Kerr Scott to the U.S. Senate in 1949, Graham was defeated in the senatorial primary a year later in one of the most acrimonious campaigns in the state's history. His detractors portrayed him and the university as subversive advocates of Communism and racial radicalism.

At bottom, then, the enactment of the Speaker Ban Act in June 1963 was the outgrowth of long-standing differences over race and the future direction of the state. Over time, the university had become a symbol of progressive social change, prizing intellectual freedom and the belief that the constitutional rights to life, liberty, and property, along with due process and equal protection, were guaranteed to all, regardless of race, religion, political affiliation, or socioeconomic status. These values, however, threatened to dismantle the infrastructure of segregation that had underpinned much of the state's political and social culture. Thus, a major purpose of the Speaker Ban Law was to forestall social change. Anticommunism was simply a political expedient for preserving the ideology of the Jim Crow system.[13]

In the fall of 1963, when the members of the active order returned to Chapel Hill after the summer recess, they wasted no time launching an all-out assault on the new law. On September 13, the active order wrote a letter to Fleece alumni to urge them "to join us in every reasoned effort towards the repeal of [the law]." The letter asserted that the law flouted the "customary trust in the members of our academic communities to analyze and discern diverse points of view" and stripped the universities' trustees, faculty members, and administrators of their "responsibility . . . to manage the educational affairs of our Institutions." Moreover, it inhibited the "pursuit of knowledge" and if effected would harm the university in its efforts to maintain a qualified body of students and faculty. "Free access and exposure to information of varying sources," the Argonauts maintained, "is vital to the academic process," and the free exchange of ideas "serves to bolster faith in democratic institutions." Frank Porter Graham responded to this appeal in a letter to the active order dated September 30. Writing from New York City, where he was then serving as the United Nations representative in the dispute between India and Pakistan, he said, in part, "I recall sitting on the platform in Memorial Hall with Democratic, Republican, Conservative, Liberal, Socialist and Reactionary speakers, and also with Fascist and Communist speakers. These speakers spoke at the invitation of responsible student groups in open forums where the speakers could be cross-examined by those attending the forum. . . . This new gag law now prohibits such free and open discussions by speakers representative of all parties, opinions and groups. . . . We should keep our forums open for responsible student and faculty groups to invite representatives of all political parties to speak on college campuses as a part of the free and open educational process."[14]

Fleece journalists weighed in, too. Virtually every mainstream newspaper in the state joined in a chorus of opposition to the law.[15] The *Greensboro Daily News,* under the leadership of its editor, Argonaut William Davis Snider, denounced the bill as "damaging to the good name and insulting to the good sense of North Carolina."[16] Argonaut Edwin Milton Yoder Jr., who was at the time an associate editor of the Greensboro paper and later won a Pulitzer Prize for editorial writing, wrote numerous editorials and articles criticizing the law. In one, he captured the prevailing objections of opponents of the bill, asserting that it was incompatible with academic freedom, free speech, and traditional values; the ban—"the handiwork of a legislative cabal"—was an "imputation of gullibility to students and of irresponsibility to faculty and administrators," and it "weakened" the state's institutions by "undercutting their good name for free inquiry."[17]

Meanwhile, President Friday wasted no time making good on his pledge to do everything he could to oppose the law. In July 1963, he and Chancellor Aycock met with the Executive Committee of the Board of Trustees of the Consolidated University of North Carolina, which unanimously adopted a resolution to "take appropriate steps to endeavor to eliminate this restriction upon academic freedom."[18] The full Board of Trustees had first addressed the issue on October 28. At that meeting, Aycock, who was a legal scholar, painstakingly detailed the unconstitutional vagueness of each of the bill's provisions: "What is meant by a 'known member of the Communist Party'? 'Known' by what means?" he asked. He pointed out that the provision about advocating "the overthrow of the Constitution of the United States or the State of North Carolina" did not specify that it referred only to overthrow by force. "Does it include overthrow by peaceful means with respect to persons who had pleaded the Fifth Amendment?" he asked. He went on to note that the title of the bill, which referred to regulating "visiting speakers," was at odds with the text, which prohibited "any person" from using the facilities of state-supported campuses for speaker purposes. Neither students nor faculty members, he said, spoke at the university for "speaker purposes" in the same sense in which that term applied to "visiting speakers." Following Aycock's presentation, Friday emphasized another "more vague and possibly even more damaging" effect of the bill: "The adoption of a law that purports to remedy a supposed communist influence upon our campuses," he said, "has implanted in the minds of some citizens of our State the disturbing notion that such an influence actually exists and is deliberately defended."[19]

At the conclusion of the October 28 meeting, the Board of Trustees unanimously adopted a resolution that "deplore[d] this legislation as a departure from the tradition of our State." The board then called upon its chairperson, Governor Terry Sanford, also an Argonaut, "to appoint a special committee of fifteen members of the Board . . . to determine and implement measures to remove this legislative impairment of intellectual freedom and preemption of the authority and prerogatives of the Board of Trustees."[20] Sanford eventually appointed that committee on October 21, 1964. The yearlong delay was occasioned by his desire to keep the speaker ban controversy from becoming a divisive political issue in the 1964 gubernatorial campaign, in which he supported the candidacy of Argonaut L. Richardson Preyer, who was ultimately defeated by the more conservative Dan K. Moore in a runoff primary in which the 1963 civil rights demonstrations and Sanford's moderate racial views were major issues.[21]

The special trustee committee appointed by Governor Sanford, commonly known as the Medford Committee, was headed by Argonaut William Clinton Medford, then a U.S. attorney. On April 27, 1965, the Medford Committee submitted its report to the Executive Committee of the Board of Trustees, by then chaired by Governor Moore. The report stated that "despite a clear preference for outright repeal [of the Speaker Ban Law], the Committee [has] concluded that amendment of the Act [is] a more practical objective to pursue." The Executive Committee adopted this recommendation and appointed three of its members to represent the committee before the General Assembly in legislative efforts to amend the act. The full Board of Trustees endorsed these actions on May 24. Although a number of amendments to the act were introduced in the 1965 regular session of the General Assembly, none made headway.[22]

In the meantime, in March 1964, representatives from the Southern Association of Colleges and Schools (SACS), a regional accrediting agency, had sent an accreditation team to the Chapel Hill campus, where the team members heard numerous faculty complaints about the Speaker Ban Law. In April 1965, SACS representatives met with members of Governor Moore's staff and Argonaut William Archie Dees Jr., chairman of the state Board of Education, to voice the association's concerns about the impact of the law on academic standards. Dees, an opponent of the law, believed that it violated SACS standards, and the association formally reached that conclusion on May 19. As a result, the accreditation of all state-supported colleges and universities in North Carolina was in jeopardy.[23]

President Friday was by now convinced that efforts to repeal or amend the law during the regular 1965 legislative session would be futile. He thus seized upon the loss-of-accreditation threat to convince Governor Moore to appoint a legislative study commission to reexamine the law and come up with potential amendments that might be considered in a special legislative session later in the year. On June 24, Moore announced the appointment of this commission, which became known as the Britt Commission after its chairperson, David M. Britt.[24]

The Britt Commission held televised public hearings in August and September 1965. Among those who advocated changing the law was Argonaut Vermont Connecticut Royster, editor of the *Wall Street Journal,* who called the law "futile," "foolish," and "bad." Argonaut and former governor of North Carolina Luther Hartwell Hodges argued that the law's restrictions on the university could impair industrial development in the state, particularly if loss of accreditation adversely affected the teaching "of science and technology[,] which must be strengthened and continually improved to achieve and maintain the standards existing in other regional areas."[25] President Friday, at the commission's hearing of September 8, gave an impassioned defense of academic freedom, contending that universities were only "useful and effective" if they were "free from unnecessary political control." He then opened the door for a compromise. Making it clear he was speaking for himself, he said that failing the outright repeal of the law, which he favored, he would support an amendment that would vest all control over campus speakers in the boards of trustees of the state's higher educational institutions through speaker policies administered by the chancellors.[26]

During the ensuing weeks, Britt consulted with Friday to draft a proposed amendment along the lines that Friday had suggested at the September public hearing. When the Britt Commission report was transmitted to Governor Moore and released to the public on November 5, it recommended that House Bill 1395 be amended to vest in the trustees of each state-supported college or university the responsibility for promulgating procedures and regulations relating to visiting speakers covered by the act, subject to the adoption of a uniform speaker policy by the boards of trustees. This general speaker policy provided that appearances by visiting speakers who were Communists, who advocated the overthrow of the Constitution, who had pleaded the Fifth Amendment in refusing to answer any question about Communist or subversive connections or activities, or who advocated "any ideology or form of government which is wholly alien to our basic democratic institutions" would be "infrequent and then [would take place] only when [they] would clearly serve the advantage of education."[27]

As a result of the Britt Commission recommendation, on November 17, Governor Moore convened a special session of the legislature. That body amended House Bill 1395 to provide that the "board of trustees of each college or university which receives any State funds . . . shall adopt and publish regulations governing the use of facilities of such college or university for speaking purposes . . . [and] such regulations shall be enforced by the board of trustees."[28] No other amendments were made to the act. Consequently, the Speaker Ban Law remained intact, except that responsibility for its administration and enforcement was now vested in the boards of trustees. The amendment did nothing to cure the constitutional infirmities of the law.[29]

A challenge to this "Little Speaker Ban Law," as many called it, came quickly. On January 3, 1966, the Carolina chapter of Students for a Democratic Society (SDS), a fledgling student organization that never had more than twenty-five members on campus, invited two controversial public figures, Frank Wilkinson and Herbert Aptheker, to speak at Chapel Hill on March 2 and 9, respectively. Wilkinson had served time in prison for refusing to answer questions about his membership in the Communist Party and was spearheading an effort to abolish the U.S. House Committee on Un-American Activities. Aptheker, a historian and member of the Communist Party USA, had led a delegation to visit the North Vietnamese Communists in Hanoi in 1965.[30]

After consulting with UNC-CH administrators, Friday supported Wilkinson's and Aptheker's appearances so long as they complied with the specific speaker regulations that the Executive Committee of the Board of Trustees had adopted under the amended act on January 14 (subject to full board approval). Those regulations required that a campus officer or ranking faculty member preside at the visiting speaker's appearance, that the speaker be required to field questions, and that opposing points of view be represented.[31] Accordingly, Friday proposed that Wilkinson and Aptheker speak at separate discussion panels chaired by Argonaut and law professor Henry Parker Brandis Jr., who would be joined on each panel by a historian, a sociologist, and a political scientist. When the proposal was presented to the Executive Committee on January 28, however, many hard-line trustees, including Governor Moore, made it clear they would not support the Wilkinson and Aptheker visits under any circumstances. The Executive Committee adjourned without making a decision on the matter and scheduled another meeting for February 7.[32]

As trustee opinion coalesced around a hard line, mainstream student government at Chapel Hill entered the fray. Led by Argonaut and student body president Paul Dickson III, who was a close confidant of President Friday's, the "overwhelming majority" of students, along with the *Daily Tar Heel* and the campus's main speaker programming organization, the Carolina Forum, strongly opposed any ban on the Wilkinson and Aptheker visits. On February 3, Dickson released a formal statement saying that as "responsible students who directly represent the student body," Student Government was now also officially sponsoring Aptheker's visit. On the same day, the faculty endorsed the visit as well.[33]

When the Executive Committee reconvened to resume debate on the issue, Dickson addressed the trustees on behalf of the student body. An air force veteran who had served ten months in the Vietnam War, Dickson said that although he disagreed with Aptheker's Communist views and disapproved of his trip to Hanoi, the university should be preserved as an "open forum" for diverse views "no matter how unpopular or divergent." The best defense against Communism, he argued, was "a thorough understanding of it." Distancing himself from the "sensationalism" of the SDS, Dickson insisted that the UNC student body was "loyal and patriotic." "When we are called by our country," he proclaimed, "we shall answer, even in the cannon's mouth."[34]

President Friday spoke next. He characterized the controversy as "severe." He supported Dickson's call to allow Wilkinson and Aptheker to speak, warning that if the visits were cancelled, there would be "no end to vexations and contentions internally," including further erosion of student and faculty morale and even a potential lawsuit. Unlike Dickson, however, who resisted any regulation of the invitation of speakers, Friday proposed "a reasonable solution" to bolster the regulations the Executive Committee had endorsed on January 14, 1966: at each stage of the invitation process, there would be broad consultation with faculty and students, and final approval of visiting speaker invitations would be made by the chancellor.[35]

After extended debate, the Executive Committee passed a resolution permanently barring the Wilkinson and Aptheker visits by a seven-to-four vote. Among the trustees supporting Dickson and Friday's position was Argonaut Victor Silas Bryant. Then, in a second vote, the committee adopted a modified resolution, eight to three, that refined the ban to prohibit the visits scheduled in March but left open the possibility of approving the visits at some later time. The committee also voted to suspend all speaker in-

Paul Dickson III, student body president (North Carolina Collection, Louis
Round Wilson Library, University of North Carolina at Chapel Hill)

vitations until the full Board of Trustees had decided upon a uniform set of speaker procedures and regulations under the amended act. To this end, the Executive Committee appointed a subcommittee headed by Bryant to draft more comprehensive regulations for consideration by the full board at its next scheduled meeting on February 28.[36]

Shortly after the Executive Committee's decision of February 7, Dickson and Friday sat down for a quiet talk on the stone wall that enclosed the president's home on Franklin Street in Chapel Hill. This was one of many confidential meetings held between the two in the winter of 1966, during which they developed a "very unusual personal relationship," were "perfectly open with each other," and came to "underst[and] each other." Friday was in a difficult position. He was caught between two forces, the university community and the political establishment of the state, and he believed the likelihood of compromise between these opposing forces was growing increasingly slim. Dickson, for his part, was unalterably opposed to any speaker regulations and informed Friday that the students were preparing to bring a lawsuit if Wilkinson and Aptheker were not permitted to speak. Agreeing that a court challenge might be the only way out of the impasse, Friday urged Dickson to begin taking steps toward litigation. As Friday would later admit, "I encouraged him in every way I could. . . . I ought to have been fired for what I did."[37]

With a litigation plan in mind, on February 8, Dickson and other student leaders organized an umbrella organization, the Committee for Free Inquiry (CFI), as the first step toward arranging a court challenge. Two days later, the Student Government unanimously adopted a resolution supporting Aptheker's visit "on the basis of the principle of freedom of speech and academic freedom."[58] The CFI also sent a letter to Governor Moore, explaining the organization's purpose and inviting him to Chapel Hill to address the campus about why he opposed the Aptheker visit. The governor did not respond.[59]

On February 24, four days before the UNC Board of Trustees was scheduled to meet to adopt formal rules for visiting speakers under the amended act, the CFI sponsored a mass rally attended by over a thousand students at Memorial Hall. The highlight of the rally was an address by Argonaut Jefferson Barnes Fordham, then dean of the University of Pennsylvania Law School. He called for "outright repeal" of the Speaker Ban Law as a "totally unsupportable" form of "intrusion of government into the intellectual life of a university." Following the rally, the crowd walked in a cold rain to President Friday's home. There, Friday, along with Argonaut and acting chancellor of the Chapel Hill campus J. Carlyle Sitterson, was presented with a resolution that called for the state of North Carolina to "readopt the Constitution of the United States."[40]

Four days later, the full Board of Trustees adopted a set of "Procedures [and] Regulations Regarding the Appearance of Visiting Speakers Affected by G.S. 116-199 and 200." With Friday's support, Bryant had drafted these regulations at the request of the trustees' Executive Committee. Bryant's version—which *Greensboro Daily News* editor and Argonaut William D. Snider called a "step toward killing the University of North Carolina as a true university"—was crafted as a compromise by which the trustees would adopt a multilayered process of rigid administrative requirements to control the appearances of controversial speakers in exchange for which the university community would receive trustee affirmation of the principle that campus administrators were the appropriate officials to oversee academic affairs. The procedures required that proposed invitations to visiting speakers be referred to a joint student-faculty committee. The final decision whether to approve an invitation rested with the chancellor, and student attendance at any approved speaker event had to be voluntary. In addition, the chancellor had the right to require that an officer or faculty member of the university chair any appearance of a visiting speaker covered by the act, that the speaker be open to receiving questions from the audience, and that an opportunity be provided to allow for the presentation of opposing points of view.[41]

In response to the trustees' action, Dickson acted with dispatch. On March 1, he and other student leaders, including Argonauts Robert Stone Powell Jr., executive director of the Carolina Forum; James Allen Medford, president of the campus YMCA; and Eric Elton Van Loon, chairman of the Carolina Political Union, delivered to Chancellor Sitterson a written request that Wilkinson be permitted to speak on March 2, and that Aptheker be permitted to speak on March 9. Sitterson immediately appointed a joint student-faculty committee on visiting speakers, pursuant to the procedures adopted by the Board of Trustees. The committee met on the night of March 1 to make a recommendation about Wilkinson's visit the next day. Although the committee was divided, a majority recommended that the visit be prohibited.[42]

The following afternoon, Chancellor Sitterson, who had supported both the Wilkinson and Aptheker invitations, reluctantly announced that he would not permit Wilkinson to speak. He noted the advice he had received from the joint student-faculty committee and explained his decision as follows: "The Executive Committee of the Board of Trustees on February 7, 1966, cancelled the scheduled appearances in March of Mr. Frank Wilkinson and Mr. Herbert Aptheker. Consequently, even though prior to the Executive Committee action I recommended that the earlier invitation should be approved, I regard the Executive Committee's action as in effect binding in these two instances." He announced the next day that he would also bar Aptheker's address.[43]

Sitterson's explanation was at odds with the February 28 regulations adopted by the Board of Trustees, which had superseded the Executive Committee's February 7 cancellation of the visits. Sitterson in fact had the discretion to allow the visits, but he excused his refusal to do so on the grounds that Wilkinson and Aptheker had become such "emotional symbols" that their appearances might well lead to revocation of the discretion already granted him and other university administrators. He came to regret this decision deeply, saying later that it violated both his "basic principles" and his "concept of what a university should be."[44] Friday backed Sitterson's prerogative and thus advanced his and Dickson's quiet strategy to overturn the regulations and the law through a court challenge. Had the visits been granted, there would have been no "injury in fact" that would have given the students sufficient standing to bring a lawsuit.

When he learned of Chancellor Sitterson's decision on the afternoon of March 2, Dickson was elated. "Man, we've got 'em now!" he exclaimed, and he telephoned Argonaut McNeill Smith to report the good news. Smith, a prominent Greensboro lawyer, had undertaken, without charge, to serve as lead counsel in advising Dickson and the student leadership about orchestrating a court challenge. Dickson told reporters that he and his fellow students would "file suit as soon as we can."[45]

But there was more to do before the case would be in the best posture for a court test. Sitterson's formal announcement that Wilkinson and Aptheker would not be permitted to speak was probably sufficient to give the students legal standing to file a lawsuit. But if the administration did not again bar the speakers' appearances, a court might decline to consider the constitutionality of the Speaker Ban Law on the ground that Sitterson had merely misconstrued the effect of the trustees' regulations. The students' legal strategy was, therefore, to force the administration to once again prohibit Wilkinson and Aptheker from speaking after they made actual attempts to speak on campus. From the students' perspective, this strategy also provided two excellent opportunities to make a political statement.

The first of these occurred when Wilkinson came to the Chapel Hill campus on March 2. In the early afternoon of that day, Dickson, with Friday's and Sitterson's knowledge, arranged for Wilkinson to address a crowd of some twelve hundred students while he stood on the public sidewalk on Franklin Street, separated from campus by a low stone wall. In a grand scene of political theater that attracted widespread media attention, Wilkinson gave a ten-minute talk in front of a sign that the students had attached to the wall reading "Gov. Dan K. Moore's (Chapel Hill) Wall," an obvious allusion to the Berlin Wall that symbolized Soviet oppression. Wilkinson condemned the Speaker Ban Law as unconstitutional, and Dickson announced that Wilkinson would appear at 7:30 P.M. on campus at Carroll Hall for his scheduled talk, "The House Un-American Activities Committee."[46]

When Wilkinson and the students arrived at Carroll Hall that evening, they were met by the campus police chief, who had been instructed to enforce the speaker ban and had also been informed in advance by Dickson of the students' plan to orchestrate a

Frank Wilkinson *(left),* with Paul Dickson III, speaking from the sidewalk on Franklin Street on March 2, 1966 (North Carolina Collection, Louis Round Wilson Library, University of North Carolina at Chapel Hill)

peaceful confrontation.[47] To demonstrate the absurdity of the law, Dickson intended to play an audiotape of Wilkinson speaking while Wilkinson sat mute on the speaker platform in the hall. The police chief, however, politely overruled the scheme. He told Dickson that the tape could be played on the outside steps but not inside the building. Dickson and the students then led Wilkinson to Hillel House, the Jewish student center one block off campus, to deliver his prepared lecture.[48]

Before filing suit, Dickson took a second opportunity to make a dramatic political statement. Aptheker, who was scheduled to speak on campus on March 9, epitomized the kind of speaker that many supporters of the Speaker Ban Law believed most threatened the traditional Jim Crow system. Not only was Aptheker a member of the national committee of the Communist Party USA and director of the American Institute of Marxist Studies, he was also the author of *American Negro Slave Revolts* and an authority on slave rebellion in the antebellum South. The original title of his speech was "The Negro Movement—Reform or Revolution?"— a topic that was certain to inflame many of the state's political conservatives.[49]

Shortly after noon on March 9, Dickson and other student leaders escorted Aptheker, who was wired for sound by a national television network, to the base of a statue of a Confederate rifleman in McCorkle Place, a spacious campus area shaded by ancient oak trees and bordering downtown Chapel Hill. The night before, one of Dickson's associates, Argonaut James Allen Medford, quietly advised the campus police chief of the students' plan for Aptheker to make a peaceful attempt to speak on the campus grounds. The chief agreed to cooperate in the staging of the scene so long as it did not violate the law. According to plan, as Aptheker prepared to speak, the chief announced to Dickson, "Paul, I want you to tell Dr. Aptheker that if he speaks he is breaking the law." Aptheker responded, "I thought I had my rights as a citizen of the United States." The chief retorted, "You do. You have a right to obey the law."[50] Determined not to allow the confrontation to escalate into chaos and Aptheker's arrest, Dickson then directed the crowd of more than two thousand students to the public sidewalk by the rock wall on the fringe of campus where Wilkinson had spoken the week before. There, Aptheker apologized that his appearance had "turned into a spectacle" and denounced the Speaker Ban Law as an abrogation of the Bill of Rights. Later that evening, Aptheker gave a modified address on the war in Vietnam to a standing-room-only crowd at Chapel Hill's Community Church off campus.[51]

On the advice of the students' pro bono legal team headed by Argonaut McNeill Smith (now joined by UNC-CH law professor and Argonaut Daniel Hubbard Pollitt, who had written a law review article in which he characterized the Speaker Ban Law as unconstitutional "vagueness with a vengeance"), Dickson made a last appeal to the administration to allow Wilkinson and Aptheker to speak.[52] On March 14, he and other student leaders forwarded a written request to Chancellor Sitterson that Wilkinson be permitted to speak on March 23 and Aptheker on March 25. The request complied with the procedures and regulations adopted by the Board of Trustees on February 28, 1966.[53]

Sitterson delayed his response, ultimately denying the request on March 31. Within an hour of receiving the denial, Dickson filed a lawsuit in the U.S. District Court for the Middle District of North Carolina. Along with Dickson, the named plaintiffs in the suit included student Argonauts Robert Stone Powell Jr., James Allen

Medford, Eric Elton Van Loon, and Henry Newton Patterson Jr. The suit asked the court to declare unconstitutional the Speaker Ban Law (N.C. Gen. Stat. secs. 116-199 through 116-200) as well as the Board of Trustees' procedures and regulations adopted pursuant to the statutes.[54]

The argument before a three-judge panel in Greensboro became a triumph for McNeill Smith, the witty Fleeceman and 1941 editor of the *Daily Tar Heel*, who was regarded as one of the state's most prominent trial lawyers. The constitutional result, despite frivolous claims to the contrary, was clear and basic. Free speech had been impaired by state action through the language of an act, which was so crude and clumsy as to leave both obligations and liabilities under the law unenforceable. In an opinion filed on February 19, 1968, the court found the law unconstitutional, voiding it along with the Board of Trustees' regulations. The court held that "when the statutes in question are applied to the unbroken line of Supreme Court decisions respecting the necessity for clear, narrow and objective standards controlling the licensing of First Amendment rights, the conclusion is inescapable that they run afoul of constitutional principles." Four days later, Governor Moore announced that the state would not appeal the decision.[55]

In the wake of the ruling, President Friday said he regretted the "cost, time, energy and creative leadership" expended on the controversy but hoped "we have learned . . . that in considering legislation affecting constitutional rights of citizens all affected parties should be heard." Chancellor Sitterson called the controversy an "absolutely unresolvable issue, except finally in the way that it was resolved." Attorney McNeill Smith, referring to the law as "the dragon [that] didn't just curl up and die," concluded: "St. George slayed it. [The] students were St. George."[56]

The court's decision brought a time-consuming episode in the history of the university to a welcome end. The secretive act passed by the General Assembly over four years earlier had led to a prolonged battle in which many members of the Fleece, joining with other friends of academic freedom and the First Amendment, struggled in vain to rid North Carolina of an embarrassing law by political action. Ultimately, as was so often the case in those years, it was left to independent judges to vindicate fundamental principles of liberty. The sequel was no surprise at all. There was, of course, no rush to hear "known Communist" speakers on campus; such speakers had merely served as an excuse for a law that was, from the beginning, primarily designed to slow the advancement of civil rights.

CHAPTER NINE

Toward a University of Diversity
and Harmony

DURING THE 1970s AND 1980s, one of the most important challenges that faced the Chapel Hill campus was promoting harmony in a university that was struggling to achieve racial diversity. Beginning in early 1970, the U.S. Department of Health, Education and Welfare (HEW), acting pursuant to Title VI of the 1964 Civil Rights Act, which prohibited any program receiving federal financial assistance from discriminating based on race, color, or national origin, directed the Consolidated University of North Carolina—then consisting of six campuses, which increased to sixteen by 1973—to come up with a desegregation plan that would bring greater racial integration in student enrollment and employment at the state's traditionally white institutions of higher learning. The charge was to utilize affirmative action to eradicate the vestiges of past segregation while at the same time preserving the "racial identifiability" of the traditionally black institutions in the university system. The struggle between the university and HEW over this mandate lasted for the next fifteen years.[1] At Chapel Hill, the overriding effort during this period was to increase the number of minority students, minority faculty, and nonfaculty personnel at the campus in a way that would not only comply with the federal government's directives but would promote harmony in a community of greater diversity.

African Americans were first admitted to UNC-CH in the law school in 1951 and as undergraduates in 1955. In 1962, Julius Levonne Chambers, who would later become chancellor of North Carolina Central University in Durham, became the first African American member of the Golden Fleece. In the fall of that year, as in each of the previous ten years, no more than a handful of black freshmen were admitted to the university in Chapel Hill.[2]

This problem was recognized even before the federal government called upon the consolidated university to develop a formal integration plan under Title VI. Efforts were already underway at Chapel Hill to increase minority student enrollment. In October 1967, Argonaut Phillip Leroy Clay, who was vice-president of the YMCA, active in the campus chapter of the National Association for the Advancement of Colored People, and later chancellor of the Massachusetts Institute of Technology, established Carolina Talent Search, a program to recruit black undergraduates. It was funded by the student legislature and was later supplemented by a grant from the Ford Foundation. In December 1968, the Faculty Council, on the recommendation of a faculty committee chaired by law professor and Argonaut J. Dickson Phillips Jr., adopted a resolution in favor of "increas[ing] the proportion of black students in the University" by means of an "experiment with a 'high-risk' probationary admissions program cutting across racial lines," among other measures. In light of this resolution and other proposals presented by representatives of the Black Student Movement (BSM) on campus, in 1969 chancellor and Argonaut J. Carlyle Sitterson appointed a university committee "on the status of minorities and disadvantaged." A year later, he appointed two black assistant directors of admissions and established a special admissions program for minority students.[3]

The first step toward complying with the federal mandate to increase the number of minority employees at the Chapel Hill campus took place on July 1, 1973, when chancellor and Argonaut Nelson Ferebee Taylor approved the institution's first affirmative action plan. It was written by the Affirmative Action Program Committee, which was chaired by professor of law and Argonaut John Lassiter Sanders, director of the Institute of Government. The plan set goals for hiring greater numbers of minority faculty and nonfaculty personnel, recommended the appointment of an affirmative action officer, and suggested the establishment of an Affirmative Action Advisory Committee "to provide an independent, informed, and concerned voice with respect to the achievement of the goals of affirmative action." On September 14, 1973, in a move supported by the active order, Chancellor Taylor appointed four students to the Affirmative Action Advisory Committee, which was otherwise composed of faculty and nonfaculty employees. On the same day, he appointed Argonaut Douglass Hunt to serve as the affirmative action officer as part of his duties as vice chancellor for administration.[4] Hunt served in that role until 1981, when professor and Argonaut Gillian T. Cell was appointed as the university's first full-time affirmative action officer.

Chancellor Taylor was also keenly committed to improving race relations in the student body, and he urged the active order to take the lead in that initiative. As a result, on the evening of February 24, 1974, Jason Nancy Logan Haigwood presented him with the order's "Proposal for Social Change," which recommend-

Julius Levonne Chambers, the first African American Argonaut (North Carolina Collection, Louis Round Wilson Library, University of North Carolina at Chapel Hill)

Phillip Leroy Clay, founder of Carolina Talent Search (Records of the Order of the Golden Fleece, University Archives, Louis Round Wilson Library, University of North Carolina at Chapel Hill)

ed that "the University should require all freshmen to take a course in human/race relations." The proposal, which had received the backing of the Black Student Movement's Central Committee, suggested that establishing such a course would not only help to increase "understanding and harmony between [the] races" but might also further the university's affirmative action employment efforts.[5]

The next day, Chancellor Taylor transmitted the proposal to dean of the College of Arts and Sciences and Argonaut James Reuben Gaskin. The course, known as Education 9, was established as a freshman seminar in the fall of 1974 and was taught by Argonaut Edith Mayfield Elliott. It called for "small group interaction with contemporary human and race relations as [the] focus for study and discussion," with an emphasis "on increasing personal and racial awareness aimed at enhancing and improving relationships between students with varied racial and ethnic backgrounds."[6] It was offered in later semesters and was ultimately incorporated as part of other courses in the liberal arts curriculum.[7]

Three years later, the active order once again turned its attention to the theme of promoting diversity and harmony on campus. By the fall of 1977, there were 1,269 African American students enrolled at the Chapel Hill campus, representing 6.3 percent of the student body of 20,162, a decline from 6.6 percent in 1975.[8] Concerned this decline indicated that minority candidates for admission were accepting offers at universities that could afford to provide handsome scholarships, on October 6, Argonauts G. Nicholas Herman and Harriet Sue Sugar submitted a proposal for the Fleece to establish an endowment that would eventually fund an undergraduate scholarship for freshman minority students. It noted "the potential symbolic value that the Golden Fleece can provide to the University community by contributing to increasing the number of well-qualified minorities in the student population," and it stated that "because the Fleece body carries the traditional identity of the highest honorary [society] at the University," the scholarship "would encourage the sensitivity of distinguished Fleece members throughout the State as well as all individuals on this campus."[9]

The active order discussed this proposal at a meeting on October 26 with Argonauts Douglass Hunt, Hayden Bentley Renwick, and Harold G. Wallace, all administrators at the university. In addition, the order invited Professor J. Lee Greene and six members of the BSM Central Committee.[10] Greene, who had spent several summers collaborating with Upward Bound, a pre-college preparatory program designed to improve the skills and motivation of North Carolina high school students whose low-income backgrounds or inadequate secondary educations could prevent them from attending college, noted, along with the head of the BSM, that many participants in the program felt that the university was neither welcoming nor sympathetic to them. This feeling made them reluctant to enroll at UNC-CH. At this meeting, the idea emerged that the Fleece scholarship should honor the ablest Upward Bound student in each year's program. Though the scholarship would be modest, it was intended to replace a student's summer earnings between high school and college. As Hunt put it, "the highest student honorary society would, by the award of this scholarship, convey a warm and helpful welcome to a student from the Upward Bound program," and it was hoped that the gesture would help to attract highly qualified minority students to the Chapel Hill campus.[11]

Jason Boyd Stephen Toben discussed the plan with the university's director of Upward Bound, who fully endorsed it. The idea was also well received by the Fleece alumni at the Homecoming Banquet on November 3.[12] In a letter to Fleece alumni on April 27, 1978, Jason Toben formally announced the goal of establishing the scholarship and called upon the support of all Fleece members to help raise the endowment. He explained, "Since almost any Upward Bound student admitted would likely be eligible for full financial aid, the Fleece award would be considered as the capstone of the financial aid package. The award would provide a substantial motivational element for these students, recognize their promise for contributing to this community, underscore the need to expand educational opportunity at the University, and stand as an invitation to these students from fellow students to come to Chapel Hill."[13]

It took ten years for the Fleece to raise the endowment for the scholarship through the financial contributions of its alumni. Shortly after the death of Argonaut Allard Kenneth Lowenstein on March 14, 1980, the order decided to name the scholarship the Allard K. Lowenstein Scholarship.[14] The scholarship was formally established in 1988 and is administered today by the university's Office of Scholarships and Student Aid. The first award was given in the fall of 1989. Since 1989, the scholarship has been awarded to an entering freshman each year. All recipients have been minority participants in the Upward Bound program who have demonstrated special "potential for contributions to the University through academics, athletics and activities as judged by performance in high school and the community."[15] The endowment has continued to grow over the years through continuing contributions of Fleece alumni.

The order's ongoing efforts to promote a diverse and harmonious university have been consistent with its members' belief that the full blessings of learning and knowledge can only be realized in an environment enriched by students and faculty who come from all walks of life. This means that the university must not only prize the diversity provided by intellectual freedom but also diversity in the racial, ethnic, and cultural makeup of its citizenry. Just as the founding members of the order aimed to bring together the varied interests of university life, the efforts of the Fleece in supporting integration, improving race relations, and increasing diversity in the university continue to be aimed at bringing greater harmony to a more heterogeneous community.

CHAPTER TEN

In Honor of Service

THE HEADSTONE at grave 2005 in section 30 of the Arlington National Cemetery bears the inscription, "If a single man plants himself on his convictions and there abide, the huge world will come around to him." These words, which appear on the grave of Allard Kenneth Lowenstein, are from a note written to him by U.S. Senator Robert F. Kennedy. On March 14, 1980, almost twelve years after Kennedy was assassinated while campaigning for the Democratic nomination for president of the United States, Lowenstein was shot in his law office in New York City by Dennis Sweeney, a former civil rights volunteer in one of Lowenstein's Mississippi voter registration drives. Sweeney said he believed that Lowenstein and others controlled him through radio receivers in his teeth. He was diagnosed as a paranoid schizophrenic and found not guilty of the crime by reason of insanity.

When news of Lowenstein's death reached Chapel Hill, members of the order who were close to him in his student days at Carolina organized a memorial service. It was held in Memorial Hall on campus in the late afternoon of April 21. Nine speakers recounted Lowenstein's years as a student and his later service in public life.[1]

Allard Kenneth Lowenstein (Records of the Order of the Golden Fleece, University Archives, Louis Round Wilson Library, University of North Carolina at Chapel Hill)

Lowenstein arrived in Chapel Hill as a freshman in 1945, a "Jewish boy from New York [who came to know] more Southern Baptist hymns than the choir director at a tent revival." He quickly became involved in student politics and helped draft the first student constitution. After serving in the student legislature, on the Student Council, as president of the Dialectic Senate, and as associate editor of the *Daily Tar Heel*, he was tapped by the Fleece in his senior year in 1949.[2]

Lowenstein was a protégé of university president and Argonaut Frank Porter Graham, who thought of "Al" as a son. In 1950, Lowenstein went to work for Graham when he went to the U.S. Senate. After receiving a law degree from Yale University in 1954 and serving two years in the army, Lowenstein joined Adlai E. Stevenson's presidential campaign. In 1958, he began a long association with Eleanor Roosevelt, with whom he traveled in the Soviet Union.[3]

From the late 1950s throughout the 1960s, between teaching assignments at Stanford University, North Carolina State University at Raleigh, and City College in New York, Lowenstein spent much of his time in the Deep South organizing and leading freedom marches in the civil rights movement. He was also active in many other causes, opposing apartheid in South Africa and Southwest Africa; supporting refugee aid in Spain; promoting free elections in the Dominican Republic and South Vietnam; reforming congressional selection procedures in Manhattan; participating in the Democratic National Conventions of 1960, 1964, and 1968; serving as a national board member of the Southern Christian Leadership Conference and on the National Committee for Sane Nuclear Policy; leading a national "Dump Johnson" movement that culminated in President Lyndon B. Johnson's decision not to run for reelection in 1968; and working on the presidential campaign of Senator Eugene J. McCarthy.

From 1969 to 1971, Lowenstein served as congressman from New York City and led congressional opposition to the Vietnam War. He later ran unsuccessfully for reelection. Throughout the 1970s, he continued to teach at Yale, Stanford, City College, and the New School for Social Research in New York. He remained active in national politics, serving as national chairman of Americans for Democratic Action, as a member of the Democratic National Committee, and as a political advisor in the presidential campaign of California governor Edmund G. ("Jerry") Brown. In 1977, he was appointed by President Jimmy Carter to head the U.S. delegation to the annual session of the United Nations Commission on Human Rights in Geneva, Switzerland, and he then served as alternate U.S. representative for special political affairs in the United Nations with the rank of ambassador.

At the memorial service, Argonaut Richard Murphy said that during Lowenstein's lifelong "contributions to the great movements for human rights, civil rights, women's rights, social justice, and peace," his friends "ranged the full gamut of party, race, sex, and nationality from Presidents of the U.N. General Assembly to prime ministers, ambassadors, senators, congressmen, Presidential candidates, Cabinet officers, columnists, educators, ministers, and [even] decathlon champions."[4] Argonaut John Lassiter Sanders summarized Lowenstein's character and contributions in these words: "Al had more compassion for other people than anyone of my generation whom I have known. This compassion extended not only to those of his own kind or class or nation, but to all people, everywhere. He was deeply concerned with how people lived, and especially with the state of their political freedom."

He continued: "Al believed with Thomas Paine that 'those who expect to reap the blessings of freedom must, like men, undergo the fatigue of supporting it.' And so he was found on the battle lines from Mississippi to Rhodesia. By action and exhortation, he sought to change unacceptable political and social institutions and conditions, and to do so in ways that would produce civil and constructive results. He was able to enlist thousands of others in the causes that moved him. And like Frank Graham, he had an extraordinary capacity to claim and hold the affectionate support of many people who often disagreed with both his principles and their application." He concluded: "He was a superb example of the difference one person can make, acting without the advantage of high office or large fortune, but with great strength of character, intelligence, compassion, purposefulness, hard work, good humor, and determination to better the lot of mankind everywhere."[5]

Eleven years after Lowenstein's memorial service, on the afternoon of December 8, 1991, Fleece members gathered once again for a service in Chapel Hill—this time to honor James Clarence ("Jimmy") Wallace, who died on November 27, 1991.[6] In an hour and a half of reminiscence and anecdote, thirteen speakers sketched his life and service to the university and the Chapel Hill community.[7]

As an undergraduate at Carolina from 1940 to 1944, Wallace was active as a staff member of the *Daily Tar Heel* and a contributor to the *Carolina Magazine*. While earning a graduate degree in physics, he was director of Graham Memorial, which was then the campus center for student extracurricular activities, and he was tapped into the Fleece in 1947. A "true Renaissance man," over the next thirty years he earned four more graduate degrees from the university in math, history, law, and public health.[8]

Wallace made Chapel Hill his home and taught at North Carolina State University in Raleigh, where he was a two-time winner of the school's Outstanding Teacher Award. "I live in Athens and teach in Sparta," he once said at a Fleece alumni banquet. His love for that Athens inspired him to nearly twenty years of service to the Chapel Hill community.[9] Wallace served on the Chapel Hill Town Planning Board for nearly ten years, on the Board of Alderman and the Town Council for all but three years from 1971 until his death, and as mayor from 1975 to 1979 and 1985 to 1987. He led the town through the toughest problems of his day: securing a long-term water supply, accommodating the needs of a growing town with those of a growing university, preserving the downtown business district, sheltering the homeless, and planning for the community's future in a way that promoted sensible growth while maintaining its citizens' quality of life. In 1983, he was awarded the Greater Chapel Hill–Carrboro Chamber of Commerce Town and Gown Award, given to an "individual who has initiated unity between the community and the University."[10]

As "the quintessential man before his time," he was an environmentalist and conservationist long before ecology and the environment had caught on as national issues. He helped write seacoast and wetlands protection bills in the state legislature and served as president of the state Conservation Council, as vice-chairman of the North Carolina Environmental Management Commission, and as a member of the North Carolina Board of Water and Air Resources. He was a passionate and persistent advocate of stopping pollutants at their source rather than removing them later at great cost. For his farsighted service, the university conferred upon him its Distinguished Alumnus Award.[11]

James Clarence Wallace (Records of the Order of the Golden Fleece, University Archives, Louis Round Wilson Library, University of North Carolina at Chapel Hill)

Argonaut Eli N. Evans asserted at the service that "Jimmy in conversation was a combination of Picasso, jazz trumpeter Miles Davis, and a four-alarm fire bell." Evans explained: "When he reached into his Pandora's box of metaphors and gathered himself for a galloping condemnation of corporate greed or government timidity, you could almost taste the pollution in the water as he spoke. . . . He taught us that no matter how comfortable we would become, no matter how blessed with the good life and suburban ease, that one must never lose a sense of outrage. His fires were stoked by injustice, set ablaze by the human waste of racism, whipped into fury by the folly of environmental degradation, overpopulation and the peril of nuclear war. Like a Carolina Jeremiah, he wanted to warn all mankind of the risk of indifference and ignorance[,] and he did so with an exuberant passion."[12]

The Lowenstein and Wallace memorial services, though organized and attended by many Fleece members, were impromptu events that were not officially sponsored by the active order. The Fleece has formally recognized the outstanding achievements and service of its alumni in two ways. The first has been through the order's awards to the Argonaut of the Half-Century and the Argonaut of the Second Half-Century, conferred respectively upon Frank Porter Graham in 1953 (see chapter 7) and William Clyde Friday in 2004 (see chapter 11). The second has been through its Chiron Awards, given periodically by the active order in recognition of distinguished service to the order. The Chiron Award takes its name from the great centaur who educated Jason in "virtue and the arts of chivalry" before he came of age and embarked on his quest for the Golden Fleece.[13] The first Chiron Awards were given in 1994 to Joseph Maryon ("Spike") Saunders and John Lassiter Sanders.[14] The plaque each received for the honor—as was the case in later years—bore the inscription: "As Chiron was to Jason, you have been to us."

Saunders was tapped into the Fleece when he was a junior at the university in 1924. He served as editor of the freshman handbook in 1923, as president of the North Carolina Collegiate Press in 1924, and as editor of the *Tar Heel* in 1925; he was also an intercollegiate debater. After earning a master's degree in political science from the university in 1926, he taught English for a year at the Georgia Institute of Technology. In 1927, he returned to Chapel Hill as the university's first alumni secretary, a position he held for forty-three years before retiring in 1970. He received the General Alumni Association's Distinguished Service Medal in 1978, the university's Distinguished Alumnus Award in 1979, and the UNC-CH Board of Trustees' William Richardson Davie Award for distinguished service in 1989. For nearly three decades, Saunders was the advisor to the active order after Professor Horace Williams died in 1940.

John Sanders, who also received the Chiron Award in 1994, became a Fleece member in 1950. In his student days, he was president of the student body, chairman of the Carolina Forum, and student attorney general; he also sat on the Greater University Student Council and served in the North Carolina Student Legislature. After earning a law degree in 1954, he joined the faculty of the university's Institute of Government in 1956 and served as its director from 1962 to 1973 and again from 1979 to 1992. From 1973 to 1978, he acted as the vice-president for planning of the consolidated university. For his long-standing service to the university, Professor Sanders's accolades include the university's Thomas Jefferson Award in 1988, the General Alumni Association's 1992 Distinguished Service Medal, the North Carolina Award for Public Service in 1996, and the William Richardson Davie Award in 1997. He was instrumental in founding the Golden Fleece Foundation and has served as its president for many years. Most notably, he has been a mentor to numerous student leaders within and outside the Fleece, having an indelible influence on their personal and professional development.

In 1998, the active order conferred its third Chiron Award upon George Lensing Jr., professor of English. Lensing joined the UNC faculty in 1969 and later became a Borden and Gordon Gray Distinguished Professor.[15] He was tapped into the Fleece as an honorary member in 1977 "for [his] demonstrated concern for the welfare of his fellow man through his leadership role on the Advisory Board of the Campus Y and his devoted service as [Assistant] Dean of Honors and as a member of the Housing Project of the Inter-Church Council."[16] From 1979 to the present, Professor Lensing has served as faculty advisor to the order. Along with serving as assistant dean of honors, assistant chair of the department of English, secretary of the faculty, and director of the Office of Distinguished Scholarships, he has chaired numerous faculty committees on issues of academic and student life. He was the recipient of the university's Tanner Distinguished Teaching Award in 1984 and the John Sanders Award for Teaching in 2001.

The last Chiron Awards in the order's first century were given to Eleanor Saunders Morris and Douglass Hunt in 2004. Morris, the daughter of Spike Saunders, graduated from the university in 1955. She became the university's assistant director of student aid in 1964 and then served as director of the Office of Scholarships and Student Aid and of the Johnston Awards Program from 1980 to 1998. She was tapped into the Fleece as an honorary member

Chiron Award recipient Joseph Maryon Saunders (Records of the Order of the
Golden Fleece, University Archives, Louis Round Wilson Library, University of North Carolina at Chapel Hill)

in 1988 "for her outstanding leadership, both on and off campus
... on the state, regional and national levels, fighting to ensure
that financial aid is available to those in need and is administered
fairly."[17] For her distinguished service to the university, she received the C. Knox Massey Award in 1992 and the General Alumni
Association's Distinguished Service Medal in 1996. Since 1989,
she has been a member of the Board of Directors of the Golden
Fleece Foundation, serving as its secretary and assistant treasurer
from 1992 to the present. She has also been the active order's financial advisor for over ten years, and she played an indispensa-
ble role on the order's Centennial Planning Committee.

Douglass Hunt, the other Chiron Award recipient in 2004, was
tapped into the order as a junior and graduated from the university in 1946. He was active in the campus YMCA, was student
cochairman of the Eighth Biennial Institute of Human Relations,
and was student chairman of the university's Sesquicentennial
Committee. His most notable undergraduate contribution was his
service as speaker of the student legislature, where he was the
leading figure in establishing the first constitution for Student
Government.[18] After graduating from Yale Law School in 1951 and
practicing law for ten years in Washington, D.C., in a firm founded
by Argonaut Oliver Max Gardner and later headed by Argonaut
Fred Wilson Morrison, he served as special assistant to the secretary of the treasury and then as vice-president for finance and
deputy to the president for governmental affairs at Columbia University. He returned to Chapel Hill in 1973 to serve as the university's vice chancellor for administration until 1980 and then as special assistant and adviser to the chancellor before his retirement
in 2002. The Carolina Seminars Lecture Series was named in his
honor, and he is a recipient of the university's Distinguished

Chiron Award recipients *(left to right)* Douglass Hunt, Eleanor Saunders Morris, George Lensing Jr., and John Lassiter Sanders (Records of the Order of the Golden Fleece, University Archives, Louis Round Wilson Library, University of North Carolina at Chapel Hill)

Alumnus Award. An eloquent speaker, Hunt was called upon by the order on three separate occasions to deliver the annual tapping banquet address.[19] He served for decades as a de facto advisor to the active order and was instrumental in helping to organize the Lowenstein and Wallace memorial services and to establish the Golden Fleece archives in Wilson Library. In addition, he has been an inspirational mentor to uncounted student leaders within and outside the order.

The Fleece's special tributes to its own exemplify the maxim *"Non ut sibi ministretur sed ut ministret"* (Not to be served but to serve). They have been given not only in recognition of the exemplary service of the persons honored but also as an inspiration to the members of the order to continue serving others.

CHAPTER ELEVEN

The Centennial and the Argonaut of the Second Half-Century

PLANNING FOR THE ORDER'S CENTENNIAL celebration began in June 2000.[1] By the following year, the order had established a Centennial Planning Committee[2] that was chaired by Argonaut Willis Padgett Whichard and was also led by Jason Eric David Johnson in 2001–2002, Jason Scott Samuel Werry in 2002–2003, and Jason Leia Michelle Kelly and hyparchos Rebecca Susanne Williford in 2003–2004.[3]

The committee's first task was to determine the correct date for the centennial observance. As already mentioned, an examination of the order's records revealed that the correct founding date of the order was 1904, not 1903, as had long been supposed. The committee thus set the date for the centennial celebration for the weekend of March 26 and 27, 2004.[4] The committee then developed a centenary program designed to celebrate publicly the history and ideals of the Fleece over its first century, to provide a public forum for a discussion of the university's future; and to offer the members of the order an opportunity to discuss its future service to the university community.[5] The committee also called for a comprehensive history of the order over its first one hundred years to be written.[6]

On March 26, 2004, the centennial events began at 6:00 P.M. in the packed auditorium of Hill Hall on campus.[7] After welcoming remarks by Jason Leia Kelly, Chancellor James Moeser, and Argonaut Willis Whichard, Argonaut William Woodard McLendon, professor emeritus of pathology and laboratory medicine, introduced Francis S. Collins to deliver the Frank Porter Graham Lecture on Excellence.[8] Collins, director of the National Human Genome Research Institute and a codiscoverer of the cystic fibrosis gene, received his M.D. from the UNC-CH School of Medicine as a Morehead Fellow in 1977. In his address, Collins characterized the human aspiration to excellence as "determination, vision, persistence, and service . . . and one surprising consequence . . . joyfulness."[9]

At the conclusion of the lecture, the active order held its traditional tapping ceremony, complete with music, Fleece legend, and the tapping of the neophytes hoisted from their seats in the darkness by stalking, hooded giants. Thirty new members (including Collins) were tapped, bringing the total number of Argonauts in the first century to over 1,700. Following the tapping, the order held its traditional private banquet for the new inductees at the Carolina Inn.

The events of the next morning, March 27, began with a public address on the history of the order by the author. Hyparchos Rebecca Williford presented the order's award for Argonaut of the Second Half-Century. She described the process by which the active order and the centennial committee had solicited nominations for the award from twelve hundred living Argonauts, and she announced that William Clyde Friday was the award's recipi-

Francis S. Collins delivering the Frank Porter Graham Lecture on Excellence (Records of the Order of the Golden Fleece, University Archives, Louis Round Wilson Library, University of North Carolina at Chapel Hill)

G. Nicholas Herman delivered a centennial address on the history of the order. (Records of the Order of the Golden Fleece, University Archives, Louis Round Wilson Library, University of North Carolina at Chapel Hill)

ent. Quoting a friend of Friday's, Williford called him "a friend to both the children and the aging" who "so dearly loves the University that he constantly prods and defends it, whether to assure academic freedom or to encourage low tuition." She continued: "He is no stranger to anyone and a friend to the most diverse set of leaders in our state. . . . He continues to set moral standards and contribute to the welfare and education of American society by his exemplary life. . . . He is a North Carolinian who exemplifies our [state's] motto *Esse Quam Videri* [To Be Rather Than To Seem]."[10]

Friday's nearly four decades of service to the university began after he graduated from law school in 1948 and took a position as assistant dean of students at UNC-CH. In April 1951, he became an assistant to the new president of the consolidated university, Argonaut Gordon Gray, Frank Porter Graham's successor. Four years later, Friday was appointed secretary of the university. After Gray resigned in June 1955 to become President Dwight D. Eisenhower's assistant secretary of defense for international security affairs, the UNC Board of Trustees appointed Friday, then thirty-six years old, as president of the consolidated university. He took office on October 18, 1956.

Friday soon faced two troublesome issues: a threat to the integrity of the university brought on by an intercollegiate athletics scandal and a threat to the academic freedom of the university caused by the state legislature's enactment of the anticommunist and anti-civil rights Speaker Ban Law. On May 22, 1961, three basketball players at North Carolina State College in Raleigh admitted to "shaving points" during the highly popular Dixie Classic basketball tournament. Friday ended the annual event, placed stringent limits on athletic scholarships, and reduced the basket-

William Clyde Friday, Argonaut of the Second Half-Century, with Rebecca Susanne Williford *(left)* and Leia Michelle Kelly. (Records of the Order of the Golden Fleece, University Archives, Louis Round Wilson Library, University of North Carolina at Chapel Hill)

ball schedules at State and Carolina from twenty-five games per year to fourteen.

From 1963 to 1966, he fought to preserve the autonomy and freedom of the university in the face of the legislature's Speaker Ban Law, as discussed in chapter 8, and in the 1970s and early 1980s he guided the university through the HEW–prompted process of restructuring to eliminate discrimination, as chapter 9 explains. In 1986, Friday retired from the UNC presidency to become executive director of the William R. Kenan Jr. Charitable Trust. In that capacity, for over ten years he helped lead major initiatives in the arts, literacy, and education. He also played a leading role in the creation of the Knight Commission, which examined abuses in intercollegiate athletics and made a wide-ranging set of recommendations for reform. In 1999, he retired from the Kenan Trust, and he has since then remained active in a variety of state and national activities.[11]

His extraordinary service to the university, the state, and the nation has won him wide recognition. In 1986, the Council for the Advancement and Support of Education rated him the most effective public university president in the nation. In the same year, he received the American Council on Education's Distinguished Service Award for Lifetime Achievement. In 1996, he received the World Citizen Award. In 1997, he was the recipient of the National Humanities Medal. In 1999, the American Academy for Liberal Education conferred upon him its first Jacques Barzun Award. When he was named Argonaut of the Second Half-Century, he dedicated the award to the ten Argonauts who were tapped with him into the order in 1948.

After the presentation of the Argonaut of the Second-Half Century award, Argonaut Richard Judson Richardson, former UNC-

CH provost and Burton Craige professor of political science emeritus, moderated a two-hour panel discussion and public-comment session entitled "A Vision of the University's Future."

Julius Levonne Chambers, Argonaut and director of the UNC-CH School of Law's Center for Civil Rights, emphasized the continuing need to ensure that minorities throughout the state maintain access to the university. While noting that the Chapel Hill campus had made "significant progress" toward this goal over the years, he stressed that the school is still perceived as being a predominantly white institution in the eyes of many minorities. Because "diversity is a great teaching tool," he said, the university should continue its efforts to ensure that its doors are open to all students.

William Friday spoke of his passionate interest in continuing reform in intercollegiate athletics. Although UNC-CH had to date avoided the recruiting scandals, academic fraud, and "abysmal graduation rates" for athletes that plague many NCAA Division I athletics programs, it was becoming increasingly difficult, he said, for the university to insulate itself from the overbearing commercialization of college sports. "When you have a situation where you are paying [a coach] ten times the salary of the Chancellor of the University, it ought to worry the Order of the Golden Fleece," he stated. "That's one of your assignments."

Rebekah Louise Burford, student body vice-president at UNC-CH, and Branson Halsted Page, former president of the Graduate and Professional Student Association, spoke on a variety of student issues, such as student apathy, the problem of tuition increases, and the strain on university resources caused by increases in enrollment. Both also stressed the desirability of promoting greater diversity in the student body by boosting the enrollment of

Panelists for "A Vision of the University's Future." *Left to right,* Herbert Holden Thorp, William Clyde Friday, Judith W. Wegner, Julius Levonne Chambers, Richard Judson Richardson, Rebekah Louise Burford, Branson Halsted Page, and James H. Johnson Jr.
(Records of the Order of the Golden Fleece, University Archives, Louis Round Wilson Library, University of North Carolina at Chapel Hill)

international students and students from different socioeconomic backgrounds.

James H. Johnson, director of the Urban Investment Strategies Center and William Rand Kenan Jr. distinguished professor of management at the UNC-CH Kenan-Flagler Business School, spoke of the pressures "economic globalization" has put on the state and the need to teach greater entrepreneurial skills to prevent "off-shore outsourcing of white-collar jobs." Herbert Holden Thorp, UNC-CH professor of chemistry and director of the Morehead Planetarium and Science Center, warned: "We can't have a world that creates technology without knowing what to do with it." He emphasized the need for greater communication between scientists and scholars in other academic disciplines so that meaningful applications of new technologies can keep pace with technological advances.

Judith W. Wegner, chair of the faculty, professor of law, and former dean of the UNC-CH School of Law, concluded the panel discussion by emphasizing the challenge the university would face in replacing the nearly 40 percent of its faculty who will retire within the next decade. She suggested that the faculty's penchant for replicating itself with scholars dedicated to the pursuit of knowledge would need to accommodate new educational demands not only in specialized fields but also in the overriding responsibility of the university to educate good citizens. To meet this challenge and those raised by the other panelists, she urged the audience and all in the university community to participate in more frequent dialogues about the university's future. For the remainder of the morning session, Argonaut Dick Richardson fielded questions and comments from the audience.[12]

The remaining centennial events were for Fleece members

Panelists for "The Future of the Order of the Golden Fleece." *Left to right,* Joel Lawrence Fleishman, Thomas Willis Lambeth, Phillip Leroy Clay, Rebecca Erin Hockfield, Eric David Johnson, Howard Nathaniel Lee, Charles Batcheller Neely Jr., and Sallie Shuping Russell.

(Records of the Order of the Golden Fleece, University Archives, Louis Round Wilson Library, University of North Carolina at Chapel Hill) only. After a private luncheon, the members held a panel discussion and general membership discussion titled "The Future of the Order of the Golden Fleece." After brief remarks from each of the panelists, there was a general discussion among the members about various ways in which the Fleece alumni might be more active as a group in keeping abreast of and acting upon issues affecting the welfare of the university.[13]

Hundreds of Fleece alumni and guests attended the centennial celebration,[14] and the public events were well attended by others in the university community. As the Centennial Planning Committee had envisioned, the observance marked an opportunity for the order to tap the last members of its first century in a grand ceremony inspired by a distinguished speaker. It was an opportunity to share with the university community the history and mission of the order and to begin a dialogue about creating a vision for the university's future. And it was an opportunity for Fleece members from near and far to renew their commitment to the order and to the university, consistent with the ideals of their forebears one hundred years ago.

CHAPTER TWELVE

The Legacy

WHEN, IN THE EIGHTEENTH CENTURY, North Carolina located the nation's first public university in the center of the state, it chose a place called New Hope Chapel Hill. In the late spring of 1904, the university's 109th year, the founding members of the Order of the Golden Fleece, the oldest university leadership honorary society in the nation, were part of a student body that had grown to 625.[1] Just four decades after the Civil War, the university's classically based curriculum had been reorganized to include new fields of study that would allow its students to meet the changing needs of the Tar Heel state. Student life had dramatically expanded. In addition to the prestigious Philanthropic and Dialectic literary societies, which had existed since 1795, campus activities had proliferated to include some thirty different student organizations. The result was a community that had become fractured by an atmosphere of disunity, factionalism, and disharmony.

The Fleece founders viewed their university as something greater than an institution of higher learning. To them, the word "university" was rooted in the Latin *universitas*—meaning the whole, or the bringing together of all parts into a unified whole.[2]

This concept of universality was nowhere better put than in Professor Horace Williams's June 1904 *Tar Heel* article about the founding of the order. "As we saw it," Williams wrote, "the problem was to restore unity to college life." He continued: "When the leaders of college life in all its interests are brought together, each must come to know the strength of the other and be helped. Thus a larger view of life must prevail here and a deeper, broader sympathy. Artificial standards must go. . . . Deep, broad and magnificent must be the flow of University life. True, and good and beautiful must be the typical University man. For all the forces in our life work together for him in eternal unity and peace. This is the ideal of the Golden Fleece."[3]

This noble and abstract formulation of "the ideal of the Golden Fleece" should not be misunderstood to mean that the order, then or now, prescribed any particular ideology or theology either in selecting its members or in exercising its mission. None of the order's successive constitutions has mentioned religion, politics, race, sex, or national origin as a prerequisite for membership. Nor were they standards by which to measure the work of the order or that of any of its members. Rather, the principles of paramount importance were that each member be a person of outstanding personal integrity and have a superlative record of achievement in service and loyalty to the university.[4] Apart from these qualifications and an abiding belief in the self-evident and universal virtues of unity and peace, members were free to believe in and to pursue any calling of their choice or creation.

The legend of Jason and the Golden Fleece symbolizes other attributes of the order's ideal: courage and comradeship in adversity, steadiness and steadfastness in the face of challenge, fidelity in times of difficult duty, and commitment and perseverance in a quest for worthy service. That Jason's story, in its end, recounts tragedy and disgrace teaches a further lesson—the wisdom of humility.

The founding members felt that their ideal of a greater union and deeper communion was essential to the fulfillment of their school's motto, *Lux Libertas*. To them, there could be no light in the darkness of division, no liberty in the chaos and rancor of narrow student competitiveness or irresponsibility. The order's founders believed also that light and liberty could only flourish in a university that embraced intellectual freedom and promoted harmony in an environment rich with diversity. And they coveted for Fleece members, in their lives after leaving the university, a continuing commitment to the noble aspirations of their Chapel Hill days.

The enduring ideals of the order are reflected in the contributions of Fleece members who are memorialized throughout the campus in the names of forty-three buildings, laboratories, and reading rooms.[5] And the many contributions of Fleece members were not merely parochial. The call to service that inspired the endeavors of active order members over the years extended well beyond the walls of the university. The lives and careers of numbers of Fleece alumni have exemplified the order's expectation of continuing service to community, state, and nation.

During the past hundred years, as the size of the student body has grown to surpass 25,000, the self-perpetuating line of leaders called the Order of the Golden Fleece has persisted in quietly doing its work through all the vicissitudes of diverse university life to promote new hope in Chapel Hill. The history of the order's first century pays a special tribute to its founding members in the language the first Argonauts understood so well and imbued with impassioned meaning: their legacy, handed on through the men and women who have been their successors, finds noble expression in the words *"Conferre cum consensu ministerio omnibus"*— "To unite, with harmony, with service to all."

Directory of Members by Class Year, 1904–2004

Members are listed by year of tapping, Argonaut number, and name at the time of tapping.

First Faculty Advisors

A   Williams, Henry Horace
B   Graham, Edward Kidder
C   Alexander, Eben

Charter Argonauts

1	Stewart, Roach Sidney	6	Russell, Charles Phillips
2	Herring, Robert Withington	7	Jacocks, William Picard
3	Robins, Sidney Swain	8	Fisher, William
4	Haywood, Alfred Williams, Jr.	9	Graham, Neill Ray
		10	Cox, Albert Lyman
5	Harper, Ralph Moore	11	Gordon, William Jones

1904

12	Carr, Claiborn McDowell	16	Barnhart, Charles Carroll
13	Higdon, Thomas Bragg	17	Worth, Henry Venable
14	Woollen, Charles Thomas	18	McLean, Frank
15	Townsend, Newman Alexander	19	Haywood, Hubert Benbury

1905

20	Miller, Thomas Grier	23	Bahnson, Agnew Hunter
21	Winborne, John Wallace	24	Calder, Robert Edward
22	Crawford, Frederick Mull	25	Abernethy, Leroy Franklin

1906

26	Sloan, Henry Lee	29	Tillett, Duncan Patterson
27	D'Alemberte, James Herring	30	James, James Burton
28	Pittman, Wiley Hassell Marion	31	Hughes, Harvey Hatcher

1907

32	Stacy, Walter Parker	36	Rand, Oscar Ripley
33	Logan, Simon Rae	37	Hester, John William
34	Robins, Marmaduke	38	Gunter, Herbert Brown
35	Fore, James Albert, Jr.	39	Yelverton, William Elmer

1908

40	Graham, Frank Porter	44	Johnston, John Thomas
41	Winslow, Francis Edward	45	Reeves, Jeremiah Bascom
42	Battle, Kemp Davis	46	Tillett, Charles Walter
43	Ruffin, Colin Bradley	47	Thomas, William George

1909

48	Teague, Dossey Battle	52	Hamilton, Oscar Alexander
49	Joyner, James Noah	53	Nash, Thomas Palmer
50	Crosswell, James Earle	54	Hyman, Orren William
51	Wolfe, Adolphus Harrison	55	Garrett, Cecil Clark

1910

56	Stewart, Barney Cleveland	59	Tanner, Kenneth Spencer
57	Turlington, Edgar Willis	60	Thompson, Gordon Wesley
58	Jones, William Henry	61	Cowles, Joseph Sanford

1911

62	Dees, William Archibald	64	Folger, Alonzo Dillard
63	Tillett, John	65	Morgan, Lawrence Nelson

1911 *(continued)*

66	Hanes, Robert March	69	Freeman, Robert Alexander
67	Winston, Robert Watson, Jr.	70	Teague, Claude Edward
68	Lockhart, John Clegg		

1912

71	Wiggins, Archibald	76	Mebane, Banks Holt
	Lee Manning	77	Huffman, Robert Obediah
72	Tillett, William Smith	78	Strange, Robert, Jr.
73	Rights, Douglas LeTell	79	Bain, Charles Wesley
74	Stokes, Walter, Jr.		
75	Carrington, George Lunsford		

1913

80	Applewhite, Blake Deans	86	Whiting, Seymour Webster
81	Chambers, Joseph Lenoir, Jr.	87	Webster, Felix Litaker
82	Cansler, John Scott	88	Drew, George Frank, Jr
83	Leach, Oscar	89	Taylor, Walter Frank
84	Pritchett, James Turner	90	Rankin, Edgar Ralph
85	Strong, George Vaughan		

1914

91	Eutsler, George Willard	96	Nance, Ophir Carmal
92	Boushall, Thomas Callendine	97	Newsome, Albert Ray
93	Ervin, Carl Edgar	98	Woollcott, Philip
94	Field, Bascom Lee	99	Bradshaw, Francis Foster
95	Fuller, Walter Pliny		

1915

100	Clarkson, Francis Osborne	105	Parker, John Merrell
101	Homewood, Roy McRae	106	McDuffie, Roger Atkinson
102	House, Robert Burton	107	Umstead, William Bradley
103	Linn, Thomas Calvin	108	Royall, George
104	Long, Giles Mebane		Claiborne, Jr.

1916

109	Baity, Herman Glenn	111	Mackie, Ernest Lloyd
110	Johnson, John Gray	112	Polk, William Tannahill

113 Ramsay, James Graham

114 Rand, Oliver Gray

115 Ross, Robert Marion, Jr.

116 Miller, Clyde Caswell

117 Lindau, Alfred Milton

1917

118 Armstrong, Ray

119 Coates, Albert

120 Herty, Charles Holmes, Jr.

121 Linker, Joseph Burton

122 Moseley, Robert Frankllin

123 Steele, William Trabue

124 Stephenson, William Hermas

125 Tayloe, John Cotten

126 Tennent, Charles Galliard

127 DeRosset, Robert Cowan

128 York, William Marvin

129 Bryant, Victor Silas

130 Holding, Graham Davis

1918

131 Bynum, Jefferson Carney

132 Eaton, William Clement

133 Feimster, Walter Connor, Jr.

134 Gooding, Nathan Green

135 Powell, John William
     Gordon

136 Rondthaler, Theodore
     Edward

137 Hodges, Luther Hartwell

1919

138 Joyner, Claude Reuben

139 Lindsey, Edwin Samuel

140 Mobley, Nathan

141 Spruill, Corydon Perry

142 White, Edwin Emerson

143 Wolfe, Thomas Clayton

1920

144 Bobbitt, William Haywood

145 Grant, Daniel Lindsey

146 Harrell, Beemer Clifford

147 Kerr, John Hosea, Jr.

148 Shaw, John Duncan

149 Shepard, Frederick Carlyle

150 Washburn, John Pipkin

151 Chase, Harry Woodburn

152 Liipfert, Benjamin Bailey

153 Lowe, Frank Robbins

1921

154 Hill, George Watts, Sr.

155 Horner, William Edwin

156 Jacobi, David Beuthner

157 McLean, Joseph Altira

158 Phipps, Luther James

159 Porter, Garland Burns

160 Williams, C. J.

1922

161	Moore, Clifton Leonard	167	Smith, Calvin Upshur
162	Nash, Marion W.	168	Wade, Julius Jennings
163	Rives, Edwin Earle	169	Young, Victor Vernon
164	McDonald, Angus Morris	170	Llewellyn, Clement Manly
165	McGee, Alan Marshall		
166	Poindexter, Charles Crawford		

1923

171	Morris, Roy Wilson	176	Hartsell, Earle Horace
172	Carmichael, Richard Cartwright	177	Hampton, George Coggin, Jr.
173	Gwynn, William Wardlaw	178	Purser, Jone R., Jr.
174	Colton, Cullen Bryant	179	Allsbrook, Julian Russell
175	Everett, James Legrand	180	Parker, John Johnson

1924

181	Bonner, Merle Dumont	186	Saunders, J. Maryon
182	Fuller, Henry R.	187	Shackell, Aubrey Earle
183	Thorpe, Richard Young	188	Cocke, William Johnston
184	Deyton, John Wesley	189	Lineberger, Henry Abel
185	Hawkins, James E.		

1925

190	Murphy, Spencer	196	Pipkin, W. Benton
191	Jonas, Charles Raper, Sr.	197	Parker, Henry N.
192	Cobb, John Blackwell	198	Fordham, Jefferson Barnes
193	Couch, William T.	199	Lineberger, J. Harold
194	Underwood, W. Emmett	200	McIver, Herman Martin
195	Watt, Lawrence Eugene		

1926

201	Hackney, Bunn Washington, Jr.	204	Crissman, Walter E.
		205	Glenn, John Frazier, Jr.
202	Raney, R. Beverly, Sr.	206	Kyser, James Kay
203	Warren, Addison Exum	207	Whisnant, Manly Dowell

1927

208	Hudgins, D. Edward, Sr.		213	Chappell, Sidney G.
209	Cameron, Edward Alexander		214	Allison, John Orr
			215	McPherson, Rufus Alexander
210	Johnston, Samuel Nash			
211	Wilkins, Robert Wallace		216	Elliott, Galen
212	Ashby, Judson Frank		217	Brown, John Fuller

1928

218	Gray, Robert McDonald		224	Morris, W. Worth
219	Adams, Lionel Price		225	Barwick, Killian
220	Spearman, Walter Smith		226	Waddell, Charles Edward
221	Davis, John Conrad		227	Bobbitt, Joseph Rosser, Jr.
222	Satterfield, Henry C., Jr.		228	Pritchett, Hoyt Baker
223	Strudwick, Shepperd		229	Gardner, Oliver Max

1929

230	Farris, Ray Simpson, Jr.		235	Greene, Ralph Cordell
231	Gray, Gordon		236	Adams, Junius Greene, Jr.
232	Galland, Harry Joseph		237	Maus, James Reginald
233	Henderson, John Middleton		238	Williams, James William
234	Brown, Travis T.		239	Holder, Glenn Parran

1930

240	Hamer, Edward Ryan		245	Dunn, William Clyde
241	Eagles, Joseph Colin, Jr.		246	Alexander, Marion Romaine, Sr.
242	Harper, William Lacy, Sr.			
243	Patterson, Henry Newton		247	Allen, Arch Turner
244	Goodridge, Noah		248	Yarborough, William H., Jr.

1931

249	Albright, Robert Mayne		253	Ramsay, Kerr Craige
250	Moore, Beverly Cooper		254	Dungan, John Elwin
251	Slusser, Frank Willard		255	Parsley, Robert Aubrey, Jr.
252	Hobgood, Hamilton H.			

1932

256	Stevens, Henry Leonidas, Jr.	262	Wright, Lenoir Chambers
257	Davis, Archibald K.	263	McClure, David Craig
258	Weeks, O. Haywood, Sr.	264	Watkins, Thomas Henry
259	Chandler, Stuart McVeigh	265	McKee, William Wakefield
260	Hines, Wilmer Moore	266	Davis, J. Holmes, Jr.
261	Rose, Charles G., Jr.	267	Alexander, Thomas Willis

1933

268	Ehringhaus, John C. B.	274	O'Neil, John Tettemer
269	Weathers, Virgil Stowe	275	Barnett, Robert W.
270	Shoemaker, Donald C.	276	Brandt, George Fred
271	Dameron, Emerson Penn	277	Daniel, E. Clifton, Jr.
272	Barnes, Bennett Harper	278	Carr, Clairborn
273	Parsley, Henry Nutt, Sr.		McDowell, Jr.

1934

279	Aitken, Stuart Chuickshank	284	Dill, Alonzo Thomas
280	Abernethy, Franklin P., Jr.	285	Andrews, Alexander Boyd
281	Patterson, F. M.	286	Sugarman, Joseph J.
	Simmons, Sr.	287	Johnson, Thor Martin
282	Bahnson, Agnew Hunter, Jr.	288	Gardner, Ralph Webb
283	Drane, Robert Brent		

1935

289	Evins, Thomas Moore	294	McCachren, James Roland
290	Rand, Hubert Hinton	295	Taylor, Herbert
291	Poe, Charles Aycock		Hamilton, Jr.
292	Montgomery, Harry Howard	296	Pool, Rufus Adolphus
293	Eutsler, E. Ernest, Jr.	297	Hammer, Philip Gibbon

1936

298	Townsend, Newman A., Jr.	303	Barnett, Joseph Yoch
299	Weaver, Frederick Henry	304	Bond, Niles Woodbridge
300	Willis, Benjamin Sheppard	305	Snyder, Jacob Elias
301	Williamson, Harry Webb	306	McKee, Donald Kennedy
302	Willingham, Francis Fries	307	Magill, Robert Nathanial

1937

308   Potts, Ramsay Douglas

309   Ellis, Albert Joseph

310   Bershak, Andrew A.

311   DuFour, Robert Brouard

312   McGlinn, Frank C. P.

313   Rabb, Stuart White, Jr.

314   Shaffner, Louis Des

315   Smith, J. McNeill, Jr.

316   Parker, John Johnston, Jr.

1938

317   Patterson, Joseph F., Jr.

318   Heard, G. Alexander

319   Jordan, William Stone, Jr.

320   Hudson, Henry Edward

321   Verner, James Melton

322   Joyner, James McMurray

323   Read, Nicholas Cabell

324   Merrill, Allen H.

325   Ivey, Alfred Guy

1939

326   Megson, Edward Heywood

327   Creedy, John Alan

328   Fairley, Francis Hilliard

329   Worley, Richard Campbell

330   Barnett, H. DeWitt

331   Hobbs, Samuel Earle Greene

332   Gilmore, Voit

333   Craige, Ernest

334   Davis, James Evans

1940

335   Gatton, T. Harry

336   Morrison, David James

337   Dees, William Archibald, Jr.

338   McGaughey, Carroll Bradford, Jr.

339   Richter, Horace

340   Green, Allen Jones

341   Lynch, John Franklin, Jr.

342   Bishop, Donald Edwin

343   Ralston, George Francis

344   Joslin, William

345   Kimball, Clyde Gates

346   Shuford, William Melvin

347   Wiggins, Lee M.

1941

348   Kline, Charles Robert

349   Lewis, Wellington H.

350   Merrill, Byrd Farmer

351   Coxhead, George Leavell

352   Cochrane, William McWhorter

353   Taylor, Nelson Ferebee

354   Severin, Paul Vincent, Sr.

355   Hobbs, Truman McGill

356   Welborn, Joseph Alson

357   Sanford, Terry

358   Tillett, Charles Walter, Jr.

359   Kanter, Edward Lewis

360   Martin, William T.

361   Hayes George Lewis

1942

362	Smith, Wilburn Jackson, Jr.	367	Baden, Thomas Benjamin
363	Gambill, Ira Samuel	368	Whitaker, Frank Ridley
364	Taylor, Isaac M.	369	Harris, Louis
365	Long, T. W. M., Jr.	370	Thorp, John Daniel
366	Harward, Vernon Judson, Jr.	371	Moll, Henry Mario

1943

372	Osborne, Henry Plant, Jr.	383	Karres, Steve Matthew
373	Snyder, Ben McClellan, III	384	Adler, Richard
374	Hammond, George Denman	385	Kilpatrick, W. Terrell, Jr.
375	Peck, J. Stevenson	386	Damtoft, Walter Atkinson
376	Meyer, Sylvan Hugh	387	Webster, John Thomas, Jr.
377	Strowd, Roy Ervin	388	Campbell, Orville Bentley
378	Long, Willie Jones, Jr.	389	Alspaugh, J. Frank
379	Bennett, Bert Lester, Jr.	390	Davis, James Rowlette
380	Carruth, Hayden	391	Burleigh, Robert Norton
381	Robinson, John Moseley, Jr.	392	Peel, Elbert Sidney, Jr.
382	Spence, Robert Atwell, Sr.		

1944

393	Bishopric, Karl, Jr.	399	Davis, John Owen
394	Newsome, James Frederick	400	Fitch, John S., Sr.
395	Thompson, W. Reid	401	White, Harvey O'Neal
396	Avera, Thomas A.	402	Wideman, Frank James, Jr.
397	Benbow, Charles Frank	403	Vance, Charles Fogle, Jr.
398	Carter, W. Horace	403a	Lanier, Edwin Sidney

1945

404	Crisp, William Thomas	408	Hunt, Douglass
405	Emack, Edward Franklin	409	McNeely, William Fennell
406	Ford, Richard Bramley	410	Tripp, William Jennings
407	Hooper, Lawrence Lewis		

1946

411	Booth, James Henry	414	Fenhagen, F. Weston
412	Broadfoot, Winston	415	Flagler, Frederick James, Jr.
413	Dorsett, J. Dewey, Jr.	416	Fulton, Charles Lester

1946 *(continued)*

417	Howell, Almonte Charles, Jr.	421	Paxton, Robert James
418	McLendon, Lennox Polk, Jr.	422	Pully, Morris Wiley
419	Maass, H. Gustav	423	Lefler, Hugh Talmage
420	Murchison, Wallace Carmichael	424	Russell, Harry Kitsun
		425	Hood, Archibald Addrew

1947

426	Stockton, Robert Gray, Sr.	434	Woestendiek, William J.
427	Crone, Ernest George	435	O'Neall, John Schofield, Jr.
428	Wallace, James Clarence	436	Eller, Thomas Robert, Jr.
429	Jefferies, Raymond Lewis, Jr.	437	Hanft, Frank William
430	Strayhorn, Ralph Nichols, Jr.	438	Kelly, J. Patrick
431	Black, Kenneth, Jr.	439	Warren, Charles Frederic
432	Taylor, William West	440	McCoy, Donald Whitfield
433	Miller, William Houston		

1948

441	Szafaryn, Leonard Adoph	447	Dedmond, Jesse Henry
442	Tate, William Knox, Sr.	448	Venable, C. Scott, Jr.
443	Sherrill, Basil Lamar	449	Kirkland, John Alvin
444	House, Ernest Jones	450	Coulter, William Robert
445	Friday, William Clyde	451	Fetzer, Robert Allison
446	Brenengen, Wayne Kenneth		

1949

452	Landreth, Monroe Mitchell	462	Carmichael, William Donald, III
453	Lowenstein, Allard Kenneth		
454	Walker, Richard Isley	463	Leary, Joseph Clarence, Jr.
455	Harris, W. Page, Jr.	464	Justice, Charles
456	Joyner, Edward Grey, Jr.	465	Andrews, Harold Lee
457	Harrison, William Sherman, Jr.	466	Sobel, David E.
		467	Mackie, William E.
458	Kirkland, Robert Edward, Jr.	468	Berryhill, Walter Reece
459	Magill, Samuel Hays	469	Johnston, Charles Louis, Jr.
460	Seixas, E. Victor, Jr.	470	Moose, Roy Clifton
461	Gordon, Richard Edmund Jr.	471	Pritchard, William Grady,

[154]

1950

472	Gardner, Oliver Max, Jr.	478	Gwynn, James Minor
473	Holsen, Roy Walter	479	Young, William Frederick
474	Gibson, Charles Robert	480	Bartlett, Charles Samuel, Jr.
475	Washington, Edward Kuykendall	481	Fussell, Theodore James
		482	Roth, William Stanley
476	Daye, Anies Raphael, Jr.	483	Sanders, John Lassiter
477	Cornish, Andrew, Jr.	484	Sper, Norman Leopold, Jr.

1951

485	Yates, Herbert Seawell	494	Wilson, James Wood
486	Stacy, Horace Edney, Jr.	495	Murphy, Richard James F.
487	Talley, Banks Cooper, Jr.	496	Vaden, H. Taylor
488	Holmes, Urban Tigner, III	497	Botto, Larry Francis
489	Jenrette, Richard Hampton	498	Bilpuch, Edward George
490	Cash, William Davis	499	McIntyre, James Herbert
491	Bunting, Richard Fry	500	Brandis, Henry Parker, Jr.
492	Woodhouse, Edward James	501	Leonard, Colvin Theodore, Jr.
493	Payne, Robert Benjamin		

1952

502	Scroggs, Robin Jerome	513	Shupine, Jerry Monroe
503	Milledge, Allan Francis	514	Lamm, James Louis DeLay
504	Wolf, William Thomas	515	Robinson, John H., Jr.
505	Love, Edgar, III	516	Henderson, Archibald
506	Barton, Kenneth Houston	517	Somerville, Paul Noble
507	DuVal, Thomas Edward	518	Bowers, Henry
508	Schnorrenberg, John Martin	519	Prengnall, William S.
509	Odum, Howard Washington	520	Thomason, Robert Hume
510	Mason, Julian Dewey, Jr.	521	Carroll, Thomas Lawrence, Jr.
511	Carroll, Dudley Dewitt		
512	Allston, Frank James	522	Stevens, Edward Amos

1953

523	Neill, Rolfe	527	Gross, Edward Bailey
524	Seymour, Thaddeus	528	Haney, James Lawton, Jr.
525	Gorham, Robert D., Jr.	529	Bell, James Andrew
526	Rezzuto, Thomas Anthony, Jr.	530	Dear, Walter Moore, II
		531	Oberdorfer, Eugene, II

532	Penegar, Kenneth Lawing	535	McLeod, James Carlisle, Jr.
533	Perrow, W. Stephen	536	Marsh, Gilbert Ernest
534	Sully, Thomas Alfred	537	Likins, Paul Ross

1954

538	Adams, James Ervin, Jr.	545	Creasy, Thomas Claiborne,
539	Lowet, Henry Augustus		Jr.
540	McLeod, George Holliday	546	Gurley, Walter Dallas, Jr.
541	Cook, T. Eugene	547	Morehead, John Motley
542	Myers, Kenneth M.	548	Kuralt, Charles Bishop
543	Browne, Herbert Howard, Jr.	549	Jordan, Lemuel Russell
544	Horton, Phineas E., III	550	Pawlik, Harry

1955

551	Taylor, Tyre Crumpler	559	Taylor, Raymond Mason
552	Potter, Edward Lex	560	Muntzing, Lewis Manning
553	Venters, Carl Vernon, Jr.	561	Forester, J. Gordon, Jr.
554	McLendon, William	562	Yoder, Edwin Milton, Jr.
	Woodard	563	Yarborough, Charles Hill, Jr.
555	Tillman, Rollie, Jr.	564	Jordan, Ralph Martin, Jr.
556	Pruitt, Kenneth Melvin	565	Webb, Richard Beverly
557	Ayscue, E. Osborne, Jr.		Raney
558	Baker, Richard Henry, Jr.	566	Fleishman, Joel Lawrence

1956

567	Vayda, Jerome Joseph	576	Turner, James Reginald
568	Graham, William Edgar, Jr.	577	Wells, Samuel Fogle, Jr.
569	Young, Robert Terry	578	Long, William Ray
570	Cotton, Guyte McCord	579	Powledge, Fred
571	Bryan, Norwood Eason, Jr.	580	Veazey, P. Burt
572	Exum, James Gooden, Jr.	581	Kraar, Louis
573	Gnanadesikan, Ramanathan	582	Katzenstein, Charles J., Jr.
574	Lambeth, Thomas Willis	583	Epps, Preston Herschel
575	Dearman, Henry Hursell		

1957

584	Sutton, Edward Wike	598	Fitz-simons, Foster
585	Oppenheimer, Jerry L.	599	Evans, Robert Mayer
586	Bass, Eddie Covingoton	600	Cunningham, Robert Joseph
587	Evans, Eli N.	601	Ludwig, John McKay
588	Kearnes, Thomas Francis, Jr.	602	Farmer, C. Douglas
		603	Wilson, Louis Round
589	Ragsdale, George Robinson	604	Chamblee, James Monroe
590	Sneden, John Aitken, Jr.	605	Brennan, Peter Joseph
591	Poteat, William H.	606	Eargle, Zane Emerson
592	Pate, W. Snyder	607	McGuire, Frank J.
593	Rosenbluth, Leonard Robert	608	Whitelock, Harry Earl
594	Beatty, James Tully	609	Freeman, James A.
595	Patterson, Robert B., Jr.	610	Daniels, Jonathan Worth
596	Strassler, Paul Gene	611	Hodges, Luther Hartwell, Jr.
597	Hallford, Edward Ulysses, Jr.	612	Green, Paul Eliot
		613	Quigg, Joseph Francis

1958

614	Payne, Roland William, Jr.	620	Peck, Harvey
615	Tillman, C. Hunter	621	Brooks, John Charles
616	Whitty, John Christopher	622	Whitaker, John Clarke, Jr.
617	Bosissavit, Jean Pierre	623	Schinhan, Jan Philip
618	Hinson, Robin Ledbetter	624	Ashford, Charles Hall, Jr.
619	Bishop, Wayne Staton	625	Jones, Jesse Weimar

1959

626	Godwin, Herman Allen, Jr.	633	LeRoy, E. Carwile
627	Lotz, Daniel Milton	634	Furtado, Donald Atlas
628	Woodard, Paul Lindsey	635	Lohr, Lawrence Luther, Jr.
629	Scurlock, David Caesar, Jr.	636	Patterson, Hugh Lester
630	Huntington, Charles Riddell, Sr.	637	Manson, Wilton Elman, Jr.
		638	Kirkman, A. Larkin
631	Smith, Norman Barrett	639	Smith, Wade Marvin
632	Goldsmith, Albert Lewis, Jr.		

640	Cummings, John Balentine	649	Van Hecke, Maurice Taylor
641	Scott, James Martin	650	Austin, Lawrence Byron, III
642	Grigg, David Lee	651	Levy, Edwin
643	Ullman, Berthold Louis	652	Wilson, Mark King, III
644	Gray, Charles Dowd, III	653	Fulk, Robert Vernon, Jr.
645	Mayo, John Blount, Jr.	654	Spain, Jack Holland, Jr.
646	Aycock, William Brantley	655	Foushee, Roger Babson
647	Holderness, Howard, Jr.	656	Johnson, M. Glen
648	Stanley, Raymond John T.	657	Boyd, Bernard Henry

658	Farris, Ray Simpson, Jr.	667	Campbell, George
659	Black, Stanley Warren, III		Worth, Jr.
660	Leavitt, Sturgis Elleno	668	Price, David Eugene
661	Sayers, William Floyd	669	Whichard, Willis Padgett
662	Patterson, Henry Newton, Jr.	670	Gump, Louis Haynes
663	Rush, Lewis Odis, Jr.	671	Tennille, Norton
664	Frankfort, Hans Randolph		Fortune, Jr.
665	Womack, Nathan Anthony	672	Lotz, Denton
666	Himes, Charles Farris	673	Taylor, George V.

674	Bilbro, Robert Hodges	684	Anderson, Frederick
675	Wheless, Dwight Hernard		Randolph, Jr.
676	Burnett, Timothy Brooks	685	Cronenberg, Allen
677	Hargrove, Wade		Thomson, Jr.
	Hampton, Jr.	686	Everett, Grover
678	Vinroot, Richard Allen		Woodrow, Jr.
679	Harriss, William Graham	687	Fetner, L. Jackson, II
680	Chambers, Julius LeVonne	688	Imes, William Carl
681	Craver, Joseph Malcolm	689	Bass, E. Warner
682	Rash, J. Dennis	690	Gaulden, James Carlos, Jr.
683	Hall, Michael D.	691	Dellinger, Walter Estes, III

692	Wheeler, Grant Walton	694	Armstrong, Daniel McM, III
693	Sullivan, William Ross	695	Irvine, James Nelson

1963 (continued)

696	Brinkhous, Kenneth M.	701	Durand, H. Whitney
697	Lawler, Michael Henry	702	Mayer, Henry
698	Stubbs, Trawick Hamilton, Jr.	703	Harrington, Anthony Stephen
699	Mann, Harold Thompson	704	Shaffer, Charles Milton, Jr.
700	Gil, Federico Guillermo		

1964

705	Floyd, Joseph Summers, Jr.	714	Smith, Roger William
706	Hays, William Arthur, Jr.	715	Wales, Heathcote Woolsey
707	Cherry, Robert Lee	716	Adams, Bert Newton
708	Merrill, W. Harrison	717	Bayer, Jeffrey Joshua
709	Clayton, Haywood Monroe	718	Martin, Edward Stephens
710	Davis, Archie H.	719	McDevitt, Larry Stephen
711	Baddour, Philip Augustine, Jr.	720	Range, Peter Ross
712	Battle, Charles Henry, Jr.	721	Henley, Thomas Franklin
713	Hill, Samuel S., Jr.	722	Cooper, Bruce Stephen
		723	Spearman, Robert W.

1965

724	Fullwood, James Roy	734	Martin, Joseph Franklin
725	Sloane, Joseph C.	735	Clotfelter, James Hodson, Jr.
726	Hancock, William Geremain, Jr.	736	Geer, William Monroe
727	Temple, Gray, Jr.	737	Sneed, Albert Lee, Jr.
728	Neely, Charles Batcheller, Jr.	738	Barron, Vance, Jr.
729	Williams, Willis Howard	739	Oliver, R. Timothy
730	Scott, Ralph Henderson	740	Shelburne, John Daniel
731	McGinty, Park	741	King, Malvern Francis, Jr.
732	Clark, James William, Jr.	742	Chanin, Michael Henry
733	Willard, Kenneth Henderson	743	Dickson, Paul, III

1966

744	Thomas, W. Neil, III	746	McCallie, S. Wyatt
745	Waldman, Sidney Ronald	747	O'Toole, Dennis Theeodore

748	Medford, James Allen	756	Medford, William Clinton
749	Freeman, J. Lindsay	757	Ingram, George Mason, IV
750	Ingram, John Carter	758	Hunter, Robert Carl
751	Van Loon, Eric Elton	759	Graham, William Albert, Jr.
752	Harmon, John Matney	760	Blackwell, Hugh Allen
753	Mason, Wilton Elliot, III	761	Powell, Robert Stone, Jr.
754	Little, James David	762	Maupin, Armistead
755	Meade, James Bullard		Jones, Jr.

1967

763	Gibson, Jonathan Carl	770	Beaver, Jeffrey Windsor
764	Verlenden, W. Lane, III	771	Hockfield, Steven Alan
765	Miller, William Propst	772	Meredith, James T., Jr.
766	Lapkin, David Theodore	773	Myer, Charles Randolph, III
767	Hodges, Benjamin Frank	774	Welt, Louis Gordon
768	Burton, Dudley Joe	775	Kiel, David Harris
769	Abbott, A. Travis		

1968

776	Hudson, F. Parker, Jr.	786	Krichbaum, George
777	Williams, Michael Wayne		West, Jr.
778	Clay, Phillip Leroy	787	Findlay, William Allan
779	Sarratt, John Lester	788	Branch, F. Taylor
780	Hill, George Watts, Jr.	789	Henry, Francis Eugene, IV
781	Schonfeld, Warren Hal	790	Dietz, John Edwin, II
782	Clark, Franklin St. Clair	791	Bowman, William Harold
783	Stevens, H. Hugh, Jr.	792	Patterson, Daniel Watkins
784	Lee, Maurice W.	793	Day, Kenneth Coyner
785	Riggs, David Lee		

1969

794	Farris, Charles Patrick, Jr.	800	Courtney, William Bradford
795	Morgan, Douglas Willans	801	Haber, John Lawrence
796	Callan, John Garling	802	Shedd, Joseph Blake
797	Monsteller, Robert Paul	803	Bishop, E. Liston, III
798	Bunting, William Carl	804	Royall, Kenneth
799	Walker, Peter F.		Claiborne, Jr.

1969 *(continued)*

805	Smith, Dean E.	811	Miller, Howard Glenn
806	Jeffress, Charles Neville	812	Albright, S. Alan, Sr.
807	Barefoot, Stephen Glenn	813	Hawfield, W. Benjamine, Jr.
808	Darrah, William Charles	814	Dawson, Raymond Howard
809	McMurray, John William	815	Stallings, W. Daniel
810	Greene, K. Edward	816	Hull, Floyd Carol, Jr.

1970

817	Whitfield, James Lawrence	830	McKeagney, Robert B., Jr.
818	Jones, Robert Brooke	831	Brown, Peter Megargee, Jr.
819	Wann, James Creekmore, Jr.	832	Freeman, Franklin Edward, Jr.
820	Peterson, Harold William, Jr.	833	Bello, Thomas Michael
		834	Leonard, J. Rich
821	Chalupka, Edward Stephen	835	Didow, Nicholas Michael, Jr.
822	Gaskin, James Reuben	836	McCauley, Donald Frederick, Jr.
823	Gooding, Carnie Clayton, Jr.		
824	Groome, Malcolm Murray	837	Atwater, Luther Anthony
825	Cunningham, Bruce , Tracy Jr.	838	Langstroth, Leland Alfred
		839	Cleaveland, Frederic Neill
826	McLean, Jack Linden, Jr.	840	Holyfield, J. Franklin
827	Dibbert, Douglas Steven	841	McDowell, John Patrick, III
828	Manekin, Robert Allen	842	Elliott, Harvey Carrow, Jr.
829	Townsend, J. Vincent, III	843	Argintar, Ronald Benjamin

1971

844	Wicker, Thomas Grey	853	Waddell, Guilford Thomas, III
845	Hoch, Paul Frederick, Jr.		
846	Hilliker, Jeffrey L.	854	McGuire, Joseph Pinckney
847	Bryan, Harry Lee	855	Padrick, Joseph Michael
848	Kassens, William Diedrich, Jr.	856	Rooks, David Monroe, III
		857	McGaughey, Harry Stephen
849	Brafford, William Allen	858	Jost, Peter Hafner
850	LaTour, Stephen Alexis	859	Brieger, William Robert
851	Stallings, Joseph Henry	860	Patrizia, Charles Andre
852	Hall, Peter Welles	861	Adams, John B.

862	Williams, Arthur Shelden	865	Chadwick, David Egbert
863	Gary, Richard David	866	Preyer, L. Richardson
864	Gray, Frederick Pendleton, III		

1972

867	Epps, Richard James, Jr.	880	Butler, George Edwin, II
868	Preyer, Mary Norris	881	Nicholson, Britain Walton
869	Wilson, Robert Reid	882	Jones, Harry Louis
870	Griffin, William Barden	883	Carlton, Katherine Vaden
871	Strong, Jay Nelson	884	Nash, Thomas Palmer, IV
872	Miller, Charles Franklin	885	Mann, Bruce Joe
873	Parnell, Samuel Michael	886	Karl, George Matthew
874	Witt, G. Evans	887	Stevens, Richard Yates
875	Potter, Deborah Ann	888	Comstock, Lloyd Karr
876	Previs, Stephen Richard	889	Snider, William Davis
877	Loveland, Louis Joseph, Jr.	890	Armstrong, Lee Roy Wells
878	Miller, Paul Felix, II	891	Royster, Vermont
879	Reid, Lawrence Alan	892	Queen, Anne E.

1973

893	Medford, Michael Terry	907	Mask, Allen Greene, Jr.
894	Bangs, H. Hoyt, III	908	Batts, Valerie Alayne
895	Case, Susan Anne	909	Saunders, Stephen Carter
896	Corum, Lee Lovell	910	Shore, Martha Elizabeth
897	Esthimer, Steven William	911	Layton, Bruce David
898	Haigwood, Nancy Logan	912	Kastleman, Kenneth Mayer
899	Campbell, Pamela Louise	913	Cohen, Gerry Farmer
900	Phillips, Reid Lloyd	914	Kennedy, Daniel
901	Daniels, Walter Etheridge	915	Evans, Emanuel Joshua
902	Lloyd, Katherine Lynn	916	Pollitt, Daniel Hubbard
903	Alexander, Frank Spruill	917	Levin, Richard Ivor
904	Barnes, Peter Adams	918	McMillan, James Bryan, Sr.
905	Putnam, David Lawrence	[919	unassigned]
906	Pool, Michael Lee		

1974

920	Bellows, Amelia Helene	933	Snodgrass, William James
921	Wrights, Thomas Henry, III	934	Mebane, Willie H., Jr.
922	Waldrop, Tony Gerald	935	James, Reid Clain
923	Davis, Joyce Leigh	936	McLendon, Mae Belle
924	Robertson, Richard Lee	937	Adler, Christopher Edward
925	Williamson, Pamela Anne	938	Brewer, James Howard
926	Williams, Marcus Whitman	939	Parker, John A.
927	Pullen, Emma Eliza	940	Renwick, H. Bently
928	Stephenson, William Elliott	941	Slifkin, Miriam Kresses
929	Hardee, Sandra Grace	942	Gustaveson, Norman
930	Fogler, Murray Jules		Francis
931	Runge, C. Ford	943	Copeland, Archie Wallace
932	Martin, Werner	944	Hoggard, Lara Guldmar

1975

945	Marbley, Algenon Lamont	957	Mann, Marsha Benton
946	West, Thomas Roswell	958	George, Betty Glenn
947	Israel, Mae Helen	959	McAllaster, Carolyn
948	Humphries, Charles	960	Johnson, Michael Richard
	Thomas	961	Dugan, Jeremiah Timothy
949	Husted, Joseph Spencer	962	Henry, Howard Douglas
950	Reeves, Nancy Ruth	963	Whitefield, Clarence Earl
951	Campbell, Cole Charles	964	Dunn, David Evan
952	Hancock, R. Darrell	965	Adams, E. Maynard
953	Jacokes, Paul Douglas	966	Lee, Howard Nathaniel
954	Bradley, Lisa Gayle	967	Wiggins, Edith Mayfield
955	Cameron, Benjamin	968	Applebaum, Mark Irwin
956	Blackburn, George	969	Schwartz, Joel Joseph
	Templeton, II	970	Cooper, James H. S.

1976

971	Hightower, Mary Gwendolyn	975	Branch, John Grimes
972	Mathews, Robert	976	Rosenthal, Catherine Janis
	Cabeen H., III	977	Simonton, Charles
973	Grimsley, Jimmy Wayne		Alison, III
974	Campbell, Kathryn	978	Wallace, Robert Lee
	Newsome	979	Roberts, James Crawford, Jr.

980	Lindsay, Susan Battige	992	Preyer, Jane Bethell
981	Pharr, Robert Lansing	993	Baer, Donald Aaron
982	Thomas, Gary Watson	994	Murray, Alan Stewart
983	Shackelford, Susan Patricia	995	Carmichael, Katherine
984	Watson, John Dargan, Jr.		Kennedy
985	Steelman, Bennett Loftin	996	Huggins, L. Victor
986	Monroe, Andromeda	997	Brandes, Paul Dickerson
987	Brock, William Burnley	998	Ward, Richard H.
988	Russell, John Spotswood	999	Powell, William Stevens
989	Sugar, Harriet Sue	1000	Hardy, Martha Nell Zant
990	Kirkman, Roger Norman	1001	Swalin, Benjamin Franklin
991	Shirley, Lawrence	1002	Phillips, J. Dickson, Jr.
	Elman, Jr.	1003	Sharp, Susie Marshall

1977

1004	Clark, Robin Weaver	1017	LaGarde, Thomas Joseph
1005	Coble, G. Rankin, Jr.	1018	Herman, G. Nicholas
1006	Arne, Paul Harold	1019	Shuping, Sallie Murrill
1007	Thomas, Nova Rebecca	1020	Smith, Barry Lynn
1008	Tindall, Bruce McGarrity	1021	Ward, Thomas Joseph
1009	Johnson, Allen Herbert, III	1022	Davis, Walter Paul
1010	Patterson, Michele Marie	1023	Williams, David Cratis
1011	Petty, Michael Darnell	1024	Toben, Boyd Stephen
1012	Lamb, Bradley Robert	1025	Morrison, Fred Wilson
1013	Carrow, H. Hill, Jr.	1026	Lensing, George, Jr.
1014	Richardson, William Odum	1027	Fordham, Christopher C., III
1015	Shiffman, Lili Anna	1028	Sheps, Cecil G.
1016	Reid, John Coleman		

1978

1029	Sockwell, Samuel Thomas	1035	Kummel, Charles Maxwell
1030	Ford, Phil Jackson, Jr.	1036	Biddle, Ann Kellogg
1031	Peters, Joni Ann	1037	Hardy, Lonza Calvin, Jr.
1032	Owens, Raymond	1038	Moss, William Howard
	Eugene, Jr.	1039	Parker, Kathleen Ann
1033	Floyd, Elson Sylvester	1040	York, Maurice Clifton
1034	Mattox, Nancy Ann	1041	Aubry, Ralph Vernon, Jr.

1978 *(continued)*

1042	Mitchell, Suzanne Mallary	1049	Scism, Laura Leigh
1043	Brown, Craig Burdeen	1050	Parmelee, William Douglas
1044	Parks, Sheri LaDeanne	1051	Horton, Isaac Byron, III
1045	Burns, Virginia Harrison	1052	Porter, Gregory Douglas
1046	Stamper, Robert Cecil, Jr.	1053	Hardison, Dee
1047	McConnell, Joseph Moore	1054	Brooks, Frederick P., Jr.
1048	Jones, William Bain, Jr.	1055	Williamson, Samuel R., Jr.

1979

1056	Jones, Gary Durward	1070	Martinelli, Ann Mario
1057	Long, Nicholas, Jr.	1071	Mayo, Thomas Bolton, III
1058	Love, Linda Louise	1072	Hoare, Geoffrey Michael
1059	Isaacs, Hanan Mayer	1073	Alston, Charles Clark
1060	Polk, Barbara Jo	1074	Terrell, Thomas Eugene, Jr.
1061	Rowe, Susan Nell	1075	Pennington, Gregory
1062	Segal, Alethea Gail	1076	Phillips, Jim Watkins, Jr.
1063	Stevenson, Karen Leslie	1077	Heneghan, Daniel Francis
1064	Kendall, Robert John	1078	DeVine, Stephen Ward
1065	Sellers, Martha Elizabeth	1079	Cagle, Dana Lynn
1066	Porterfield, William David	1080	Bilionis, Louis Dean
1067	Mason, Karol Virginia	1081	Ulman, Cary Herbert
1068	Kapp, M. Keith	1082	Cooper, Glinda Sue
1069	Edmiston, Janice Lynne		

1980

1083	Steigerwald, William Richard	1094	Cox, Cynthia Marie
		1095	Weiss, Jennifer
1084	Weir, Heather Hope Helen	1096	Cabe, Linda Marie
1085	Ellis, Adele Denise	1097	Campbell, Catherine Jeanne
1086	Boatwright, Ronald Gail	1098	Long, Robert Allen, Jr.
1087	Duckworth, P. Frederick, Jr.	1099	Heyward, Eva Jeannette
1088	Cooper, Roy Asberry, III	1100	Kelly, John Brendan
1089	Honbarrier, Donald E., Jr.	1101	Fuse, Rosalind Runae
1090	Saunders, Robert Walter	1102	Bernholz, Dorothy Cochrane
1091	Pulver, Robin Gilles		
1092	Gray, Deborah Charleen	1103	Davis, Walter Royal
1093	Parker, Sharon Lee	1104	Betts, Doris Waugh

1981

1105 Shadroui, George Phillip

1106 Horne, Terry DeWayne

1107 Leaver, Evelyn Ruth

1108 Dean, Marcia Louise

1109 Buckner, Joseph Moody

1110 Seymour, Frances Jane

1111 Bledsoe, Louis Adams, III

1112 Montgomery, Wanda Anita

1113 Kelley, Pamela Sue

1114 Smith, Carolyn Moore

1115 Johnson, Robert Edward

1116 Leight, Margaret Graham

1117 Winston, James Horner, Jr.

1118 Harry, Randolph Herman

1119 Osborne, Gale Marjorie

1120 Tucker, Linda Rochelle

1121 Jessiman, Thomas Antony

1122 Strayhorn, Susan Elaine

1123 Richardson, Richard J.

1124 Shaffer, Charles Milton, Sr.

1125 Greenberg, Bernard George

1126 Brooks, Edwin Willis

1982

1127 Bourgeois, Nadine Marie

1128 Black, James Frederick

1129 Bianchi, Robert John

1130 Ellis, Lawrence Thomas, Jr.

1131 Ellison, Maxlyn LaVie

1132 Carpenter, Mark Evan

1133 Lanier, Jennifer Anne

1134 Detmer, William Matthew

1135 Brady, Elizabeth Corinne

1136 Keeshan, Nancy Kay

1137 Martin, ElChino Miro

1138 Sharpe, Amy Marie

1139 Bondurant, Ward Scott

1140 Henderson, Mary Josephine

1141 Gardiner, Charles L.

1142 King, Caleb Kimball

1143 Beeson, Donald Eugene

1144 Mock, Conrad Davis, Jr.

1145 Craig, John O'Neal, III

1146 Divine, Robert Carter

1147 Pentz, Alison

1148 Norberg, Scott Fredrik

1149 Bowles, Hargrove
     "Skipper," Jr.

1150 Sitterson, J. Carlyle

1151 Okun, Daniel Alexander

1983

1152 Horovitz, Rachael Keefe

1153 Plummer, Robert Wayne

1154 Hoover, Hunter Ashley

1155 Bach, Robert Joseph

1156 Walsh, Susan Elizabeth

1157 Kimball, William Hugo

1158 Blackburn, Frances Lucille

1159 Fischer, Anne Crowe

1160 Drescher, John Ernest, Jr.

1161 Mitchell, Stephen
     Alphonsus

1162 McElhaney, Jeffrey James

1163 Ennen, Elizabeth Leigh

1164 Drechsler, David Edwin

1165 Staton, Lisa Anne

1166 Shiver, Gerrie Michelle

1167 Cumpsty, J. Michael

1168 Vandenbergh, Michael Paul

1983 *(continued)*

1169	Moore, Valerie Lynn	1174	Beeson, Anne Milton
1170	Perkins, Samuel Bruce	1175	Leutze, James R.
1171	Latham, Vicki LeGrand	1176	Massey, Charles Knox, Sr.
1172	DeVine, Mary Patricia	1177	Hunt, James Baxter, Jr.
1173	Chiu, Julie Christine		

1984

1178	Irvine, Edward Claywell	1190	McCoy, David Timothy
1179	Robinson, LaQuetta Ann	1191	Owens, Richard David
1180	Stumpf, Andrea Emily	1192	Wilson, John Bernhardt, Jr.
1181	Brown, Tresa Suzette	1193	Baxter, Edith Maria
1182	Johnson, Keith Harrison	1194	D'Amico, Joseph Allen
1183	Parker, Paul Gray	1195	Mewborne, W. Burke, III
1184	Sullivan, Timothy Patrick	1196	Halpern, Lucia Veronica
1185	Maslia, David Jeffrey	1197	Jones, Mary Margaret
1186	Jordan, Michael Jeffrey	1198	Byrd, Robert Gray
1187	Wulfhorst, Debra Lynn	1199	Cansler, James Olin
1188	Exum, James Jervalle	1200	Schoultz, Lars Gustav
1189	Keesler, David Culver	1201	Percy, Walker

1985

1202	Evans, Mary Elizabeth	1216	Cobb, Suzanne
1203	Williams, Tommy Earl	1217	Macdonald, Glen David
1204	Mohr, Jack Edmund	1218	Boyle, Walter Douglas Long, Jr.
1205	Bain, Alton Deems		
1206	Biddell, Adrian John	1219	Hiday, Jeffrey Lee
1207	Smith, Albertina Denise	1220	Banks, Sherrod
1208	Stinneford, Mark Stephen	1221	Urban, Sarah
1209	Lankard, Brayce Aaron	1222	King, Dean Howard
1210	Bowman, Terry Glenn	1223	Robertson, Allen Keith
1211	Balgarnie, Andrew James	1224	Jones, H. G.
1212	Kelley, Katharine Wilkes	1225	Durham, Woody Lombardi
1213	Mills, F. Fetzer, Jr.	1226	Balyora, Enrique
1214	Ofseyer, Jeremy Joshua	1227	Cell, Gillian Townsend
1215	Creech, David Capps, Jr.	1228	Pritchett, Mebane Moore

1986

1229	Tillman, Otis Edward, Jr.	1241	Rickert, Arne Joost
1230	Barrett, Vikki Jaye	1242	Berney, Philip Edward
1231	Reynolds, Kimberly Sue	1243	Roseborough, Teresa Wynn
1232	Pavao, Mark Hersey	1244	Schmidt, David Bradley
1233	Lefler, Elizabeth Ashley	1245	Bennett, Herman Lee
1234	Olson, Janet Anne	1246	Mauer, Charles E.
1235	Fountain, Edwin Louis	1247	Tulchin, Joseph S.
1236	Wilson, Michael Roscoe	1248	Bondurant, Stuart
1237	Roddy, Camille Zebretta		Osborne, Jr.
1238	Kennedy, John Lacy, Jr.	1249	Palmer, Colin A.
1239	Adler, Susan Emily	1250	Bowden, Anne Rea
1240	Burton, William Regan		

1987

1251	Jenkins, Mary Campbell	1265	Hart, Todd Christopher
1252	Hassel, Bryan Christopher	1266	Varcoe, Francesca Nancy
1253	Bell, Asa Lee, Jr.	1267	Mitchell, Jean Elizabeth
1254	Williams, John Wesley, II	1268	Zook, James Randolph, Jr.
1255	Smith, Kenneth	1269	Roach, Janet
1256	Jackson, Odessa Palmer	1270	Ayscue, Emily Urquhart
1257	Anderson, Sibby Ellen	1271	Johnston, James Thornhill
1258	Jones, Raymond Clifton	1272	Bost, Thomas
1259	Butler, Sally Marcella	1273	Little, William Frederick
1260	Maler, William Steven	1274	Schroeder, Frederic W., Jr.
1261	Martin, Scott Thomas	1275	Coates, Gladys Hall
1262	Little, Walter Leake Parsons	1276	Daye, Charles E.
1263	Childress, Lawrence	1277	Swofford, John Douglas
	Dobson	1278	Steele, Henry Max
1264	Clark, Martin Matthews		

1988

1279	Perry, Kenneth Martin	1285	Kimmelman, Robin P.
1280	Bolch, Suzanne Elisabeth	1286	Gilbert, Durral Ray
1281	Tran, Liem Thanh	1287	Kashani-Sabet, Firoozeh
1282	Carlton, Eileen Renee	1288	Scholl, Mary Susan
1283	Hurst, Patricia Lyn	1289	Mulvey, Kathryn Louise
1284	Sartain, Sophie	1290	Maechling, Claude Ricketts

1988 *(continued)*

1291	Farmer, James Thomas	1298	Geer, Caro Parks
1292	Brandon, Rochelle Monique	1299	Taubman, Andrew Bennett
1293	Barnard, Ellen Marie	1300	Poole, Darrin Maurice
1294	Donovan, Victoria Kathleen Marjorie	1301	Gebauer, Wendy Sue
		1302	Dorrance, A. Anson, IV
1295	McClellan, Lucy Dell	1303	Bolish, Nancy L.
1296	Egues, Michael	1304	Morris, Eleanor Saunders
1297	Yelverton, William Forrest, II	1305	Calhoun, Craig J.
		1306	Wallace, Harold G.

1989

1307	Hathaway, Keith Stuart, Jr.	[1322	unassigned]
1308	McDonnell, Pamela Jean	1323	Mebane, Felicia Eugenia
1309	Haywood, Kenneth Clarke	1324	Beasley, Jody Keith
1310	Tepper, Steven Jay	1325	Brown, Cedric Levon
1311	Hicks, Redell Javoyne Hill	1326	Madry, Lisa Katherine
1312	Krebs, Thomas Robert	1327	Martin, Kevin Jeffrey
1313	Riemann, Neil Alvin	1328	Cooke, Robert Cameron, Jr.
1314	Winkler, Laurie Ann	1329	Ehringhaus, Susan Haughton
1315	Thorp, Clay Bernardin		
1316	Higgins, Shannon Danise	1330	Hiskey, Richard Grant
1317	Reist, Adam Aston	1331	Kenan, Thomas Stephen, III
1318	Lutes, Jean Marie	1332	Conway, Patrick Joseph
1319	Pizer, William Aaron	1333	Whitted, Alexine A.
1320	Fountain, David Burton	1334	Little, C. Crowell
1321	Blanks, Tonya Robertina		

1990

1335	Alston, Jamesee Cheri	1344	Bates, Tracey Marie
1336	Guettel, Alexander Burton	1345	Karcher, Timothy Quai
1337	Breuss, Kristin Lynn	1346	Loughran, Joseph Michael, III
1338	Frye, Lisa Lanette		
1339	Lewis, William David Brien	1347	Whittier, Donald Andrews
1340	Latimer, Lee Winston	1348	Ards, Angela Ann
1341	Langman, James Elliott	1349	Largess, Stephen Luke
1342	Dowling, Ruth Tappan	1350	Chaney, Bethany Evelyn
1343	Crum, Catherine Claire	1351	DiGiano, Chistopher John

1990 *(continued)*

1352 Mewborne, Virginia Jordan
1353 Edwards, Fitzgerald
Clareforster A. W.
1354 Holman, James Blanding, IV
1355 Bryan, James Alexander, II

1356 Featherstone, Gerald Lynn
1357 Meyer, Thomas J.
1358 Paul, Herbert D.
1359 Hines, Judith Albergotti

1991

1360 Abbott, Elizabeth Gracie
1361 Lomax, John Frank, Jr.
1362 Couch, Sharon Renee
1363 Deifell, Anthony Stuart
1364 Moorthy, Hemamalini
1365 Burniston, Mark Turner
1366 Evans, Sabrina Dawn
1367 Tracy, Jeffrey Scott
1368 Kappel, Quaker Elizabeth
1369 Brown, Christopher Lemont
1370 Bissette, Winston Louis, III
1371 Baker, Debbie Gaurnet

1372 Steiner, Michael Newport
1373 Benton, James Claude
1374 Vollmer, Jessica Leigh
1375 Fox, Ulrich Alexander
1376 Wilkinson, Christopher
Sean
1377 Sipress, Joel Michael
1378 Choi, Seong Soo
1379 Gooder, Harry
1380 Johnson, Audreye E.
1381 Capel, Edwin Arthur, Jr.

1992

1382 Ball, William David
1383 Zucker, Nancy Lee
1384 Peeler, Matthew Scott
1385 Rentz, Meridith Leigh
1386 Lumsden, Dana Clinton
1387 Chilton, Mark Hayes
1388 Williams, Kimberly Ann
1389 Lynch, Heather Jean
1390 Davis, Hubert Ira, Jr.
1391 Morgado, Natalie Dawn

1392 Ose, Erik Dexter
1393 Stewart, Matthew Dan
1394 Pons, Christy Lynn
1395 Rosen, Eric Brent
1396 Heyd, Matthew Foster
1397 Billing, John English
1398 Hadzija, Boka Wesley
1399 Friday, Ida Howell
1400 Morton, Hugh MacRae

1993

1401 Montross, Eric Scott
1402 Moran, Kevin Sloane
1403 Philson, Caroline Bernice

1404 Forte, Stormie Denise
1405 Clontz, Diana Ruth
1406 Schwartz, Rona Adele

1993 *(continued)*

1407 Wooten, Patrick Sloan
1408 Gowda, Deepthinman Krishne
1409 Baumann, Carl Christopher
1410 Hawkins, William Lee, Jr.
1411 Thomas, Michelle Lisa
1412 Hamm, Mia Margaret

1413 Shelburne, Mark Howard
1414 Airan, Rashmi Helen
1415 Rizzo, Paul Joseph
1416 Royall, Kenneth Claiborne, III
1417 Stone, Sonja Haynes
1418 Stegman, Michael Allen

1994

1419 Smith, Timothy Cornail
1420 Presler, Myles O'Hara
1421 Williamson, Matthew David
1422 Holliday, Corey Lamont
1423 Battle, George Edward, III
1424 Copland, James Reuben, IV
1425 Fan, William Li-Goon
1426 Campbell, Ruth Maxine

1427 McCutcheon, Kimberly Erin
1428 Davidson, James
1429 Colton, Marie Watters
1430 Reed, John Shelton
1431 Spangler, Clemmie Dixon, Jr.
1432 Scatliff, James Howard

1995

1433 Maddox, Brandon Lane
1434 Edmisten, Loura Elaine
1435 Alexander, Renee Jacqueline
1436 Reinglass, Carolyn Renee
1437 Strickler, John Howard
1438 Johnston, Nicholas Simon MacPherson
1439 Liu, David Wei
1440 Carr, Russell Bryant
1441 Tuttle, Harrison Gray
1442 Venturini, Tisha Lee
1443 Shah, Sneha Champak
1444 King, Bradley Ross
1445 Kothandapani, Rupa Virupaksha
1446 Cox, Jason Ralph
1447 Oliver, George Mason
1448 Dalal, Nilufer
1449 Headrick, Nathan Paul

1450 Moore, Rebecah Caroline
1451 Cunningham, James Calvin, III
1452 Jaworsky, Tommy Joe, II
1453 Toms, Cynthia Wrenn
1454 Batada, Ameena
1455 Atkeson, Jonathan Granger
1456 Smith, Charlotte Daniele
1457 Johnson, Michelle Lesley
1458 Davidson, Stefanie Lynn
1459 Brandenburg, Stacey Michelle
1460 Huang, Jeffrey Allen
1461 Taylor, Allison Jane
1462 Hardin, Paul
1463 Stone, Chuck S., Jr.
1464 Wegner, Judith Welch
1465 Peacock, James Lowe, III

1996

1466 Hultquist, Katherine Grace
1467 Wherry, Frederick Fitzgerald
1468 Monroe, Taunya Narrell
1469 Sides, John Michael
1470 Alston, Pamela Kaye
1471 Gourdet, Nicolas Patrice
1472 Dervin, John Elliot
1473 Artis, Johnnie Earl, Jr.
1474 Chu, Grace Chia-Lan
1475 McWilliams, John Michael, Jr.
1476 Jackson, George Lee
1477 White, Katherine Faye
1478 McNerney, Katherine Seton
1479 Burke, Timothy John
1480 Matsen, Susanna Lovell

1481 Robbins, Linwood Ladell
1482 Ahdieh, Omid
1483 Sarratt, Wendy Elizabeth
1484 Koonce, Thomas Frederick
1485 Ryan, Christine Marion
1486 Hayes, David Neil
1487 Foote, Shelby Dade
1488 Tyson, Ruel Willoughby
1489 Lovelace, Charles Edward, Jr.
1490 Hile, James William
1491 Goldstein, Burton Benjamin, Jr.
1492 Allen, Arch Turner, III

1997

1493 Bright, Jerry
1494 Kilbourne, James Walter
1495 Taylor, Chandra Terice
1496 Conner, Christopher Lee
1497 Le, Trinh Thi
1498 Shastri, Kirti Ann
1499 Gragg, Heralda Mavis
1500 Watson, Linwood Worth
1501 Kraft, Katherine Lorraine
1502 Boze, Scott Hunter
1503 Nathan, Mohan
1504 Parrish, Erin G.

1505 Harty, Justin Jerel
1506 Locklear, Amy Lynn
1507 Tan, Daniel Henry
1508 Thornburg, Ryan Michael
1509 Boulton, Donald Arthur
1510 Ibrahim, Michel A.
1511 Woodard, Harold
1512 Howes, Jonathan Broome
1513 Clark, Henry Toole, Jr.
1514 Clark, Blanche Burrus
1515 Willis, Rachel A.
1516 Adler, Robert Sanford

1998

1517 Manekin, Sarah Dorothy
1518 Dilg, Helen Lane
1519 Harris, Charles Joseph
1520 Fischer, Alison Leigh
1521 Papon, Lucienne Claire
1522 Crisp, Charles Michael

1523 Gray, Kimberly Joy
1524 Werley, Cindy Jo
1525 McDonald, Raegan E.
1526 McCollum, Marc Stewart
1527 Jamison, Antawn Cortez
1528 Perry, Mary Elizabeth

1998 *(continued)*

1529	Hawthorne, Lacey Adele	1539	Fulton, Shana Laverne
1530	Williamson, Emily Lynn	1540	Barrett, Margaret Bryant
1531	Hipps, John Bates	1541	Guthridge, William Wallace
1532	Hockfield, Rebecca Erin	1542	Royster, Thomas
1533	Gilmartin, Eamon Francis		Sampson, Jr.
1534	Farmer, Eric Ian	1543	Royster, Caroline Henry
1535	Traub-Werner, Marion Ruth	1544	LeFebvre, Donna Harrison
1536	Hammack, Scott Michael	1545	Hershey, H. Garland
1537	Reid, Tracy Lashawn	1546	Rand, Anthony Eden
1538	Hedt, Bethany Lynn	1547	Baddour, Richard Allen

1999

1548	Jernigan, David Wayne	1565	Scruggs, Amy Jo
1549	Parlow, Cynthia Marie	1566	Schlitt, Ryan Edward
1550	Lord, Charles Edward	1567	Bly, Donald André
1551	Cunningham, Nikolas Ralf	1568	Moore, Monika Leigh
1552	Thomas, Kevin Clarence	1569	Warren, William
1553	Presnell, Sabrina Kathleen		Addison, Jr.
1554	Heinke, Nicholas Peter	1570	Charnaux, Christian Hubert
1555	Anderson, Patrick W.	1571	Nieman, Jeffrey Larkin
1556	McDuffie, Janora Ann	1572	Williams, Mary Katherine
1557	Luebke, Emily J. Larson	1573	Bowles, Erskine Boyce
1558	Brown, Na Orlando	1574	Leuchtenburg, William E.
1559	Grano, Megan Elizabeth	1575	Stout, Cheryl Barbour
1560	Pike, Jeffrey Mark	1576	Ervin, Archie W.
1561	Alexander, Benjamin David	1577	Brown, Jane D.
1562	Whaley, Amy Lorene	1578	Edgerton, J. Wilbert
1563	Phelps, Janey Roxanna	1579	Hatchell, Sylvia R.
1564	Look, Rodney B.		

2000

1580	Fay, Zachary Edling	1586	Ward, Zachary Joseph
1581	Patel, Nilpesh Mahesh	1587	Wagner, David Lawrence
1582	Eapen, Zubin John	1588	Fortune-Greeley, Hannah
1583	Sacks, Lauren Elizabeth		Cain
1584	Cooke, David Michael	1589	Wurth, Emily Louise
1585	Cooper, Erin Elizabeth	1590	Moore, Jesse Keith Barton

2000 *(continued)*

1591 Rentas, Lerissa Yvette
1592 Markatos, Dennis Leonidas
1593 Little, Joseph Alexander
1594 Mehfar, Ali Allexandre
1595 Simpson, Dana Edward
1596 Colindres, Romulo
Ernesto, Jr.

1597 Grossman, Glenn Eric
1598 Ruffin, Benjamin Sylvester
1599 McCoy, William Octavius
1600 Johnson, James H., Jr.
1601 Brubaker, Howard J.
1602 DeSaix, Jean Swaim
1603 Beyle, Thad Lewis

2001

1604 Eifrig, David Eric, Jr.
1605 Myers, Devon Anne
1606 Pruitt, Terry Wayne
1607 Dees, Matthew Brent
1608 Fawcett, Anne Elizabeth
1609 Patel, Sachin Rambhai
1610 Quarles, Ann Elizabeth
1611 Bell, Corey L.
1612 Florance, Meredith Grace
1613 Miller, Kristin Cheasty
1614 Schwartz-Barcott, Rye M.
1615 Higuchi, Aya
1616 Morris, William Gardner, III
1617 Lea, Rebecca Taylor
1618 Patel, Manali Indravadan
1619 Graham-Bailey, Malika
Josina Helena

1620 Triche, Jessica Lee
1621 McGlone, Emilie Pamela
1622 Parthasarathy, Bharath
1623 Kleysteuber, William
Rudolph, IV
1624 Johnson, Eric David
1625 Hunter, Kathleen R.
1626 McClure, Christopher
Douglas
1627 Johnson, John Hiram, III
1628 Brooks, Shawn Kalio
1629 Basnight, Marc
1630 Morrison, Mary Fanning
1631 DeFriese, Gordon H.
1632 Sheldon, George Frank
1633 Lane, Mary Turner
1634 Evans, John Parkhill

2002

1635 Polanco, Aidil Altagracia
1636 Pearson, Joanna Kristine
1637 Newman, Sundarkia Shanta
1638 Young, Justin Coleman
1639 Stepp, Jennifer Royce
1640 Henson, Baker Livingston
1641 Ivey, Laura A.
1642 Scott, Carmen Laverne
1643 Alexander, Caroline Austin

1644 Swinson, Davene DaShawn
1645 Kertesz, Johanna Susan
1646 Black, Tiffany Mia
1647 Thornton, David Dontay
1648 Makwana, Neera
1649 Presler, Henrietta Heiss
1650 Harvey, Marcus Donté
1651 Melvin, Lucy Elizabeth
1652 Blue, Rachel Teneil

2002 *(continued)*

1653	Werry, Scott Samuel	1662	Rupar, Theresa Marie
1654	Willett, Kristen Suzanne	1663	McGhee, Jasmine Spring
1655	Agarwal, Maneesha	1664	Thorp, Herbert Holden
1656	Daum, Jennifer Ann	1665	Leloudis, James Linwood, II
1657	Peters, Susan Rae	1666	Eubanks, Trevaughn Brown
1658	Doggett, James Wellner	1667	Luse, Donald E.
1659	Potter, Mary Elizabeth	1668	Williams, Richard Tyrone
1660	Dubé, Karine	1669	Shelton, Karen C.
1661	Hashagen, Frederick William, III	1670	Futrelle, G. Linwood, Jr.

2003

1671	Chapman, David Frederic	1686	Burford, Rebekah Louise
1672	McManus, Julie Cecelia	1687	Slain, Jonathan Philip
1673	Guterman, Lydia Harris	1688	Citineni, Sindhura
1674	Sura, Siddharth Piyush	1689	Bethea, April Denise
1675	Williford, Rebecca Susanne	1690	Ferris, Frances Anne
1676	Spillman, Amanda Danielle	1691	Powell, Deone Demetris
1677	Lanier, Gregory Ryan	1692	Schmitt, Stephanie Ann
1678	Varner, Kenneth Edward	1693	Page, Branson Halsted
1679	Terry, Samantha Elizabeth	1694	Herman, Daniel C.
1680	Phaneuf, Charles Joseph	1695	Lam, William C.
1681	Barnette, Elesha Renee	1696	Kirkpatrick, Robert G., Jr.
1682	Fjellstedt, Anders Paul	1697	Kleinman, Sherryl
1683	Benton, Kimberley Layne	1698	Curtis, Jonathan Edward
1684	Kelly, Leia Michelle	1699	Smith, Michael Rollan
1685	Angeles, David Lyndon Weber		

2004

1700	Kistin, Elizabeth James	1707	Nagaraj, Sunil S.
1701	Langberg, Jason Brett	1708	Yang, Sendra
1702	Tepper, Matthew Samuel	1709	Flanagan, Shalane Grace
1703	West, Haley Elizabeth	1710	Goodman, Carrie Elizabeth
1704	Reddick, Catherine Anne	1711	Moody, Norledia Shian
1705	Walker, Kathryn Jordan	1712	Laughlin, Jonas Blaine
1706	Veerasethakul, Vipavee Toa	1713	Houston, Conitras Mamieal

1714	Wheeler, Ashton Lee	1722	Cherry, Thomas Kevin B.
1715	Harris, Katherine Jennifer	1723	Hurwitz, Amy Samara
1716	Iravani, Heide Motaghi	1724	Nussbaum, Abraham M.
1717	Davis, Erin Nicole	1725	Collins, Francis Sellers
1718	Anderson, Charles Daniel	1726	Carson, Virginia Sue
1719	Waxman, Daniel Evan	1727	Bresciani, Deano Luigi
1720	Panjabi, Rajesh Ramesh	1728	Harris, Trudier
1721	Bushman, Jennifer Elaine	1729	Ferrell, Joseph S.

Alphabetical Directory of Members, 1904–2004

Members are listed alphabetically with Argonaut number and name at the time of tapping (cross-referenced to current name where appropriate).

769	Abbott, A. Travis	1414	Airan-Pace, Rashmi Helen
1360	Abbott, Elizabeth Gracie	279	Aitken, Stuart Chuickshank
280	Abernethy, Franklin P., Jr.	249	Albright, Robert Mayne
25	Abernethy, Leroy Franklin	812	Albright, S. Alan, Sr.
716	Adams, Bert Newton	1561	Alexander, Benjamin David
965	Adams, E. Maynard	1643	Alexander, Caroline Austin
538	Adams, James Ervin, Jr.		(*see* Williams)
861	Adams, John B.	C	Alexander, Eben
236	Adams, Junius Greene, Jr.	903	Alexander, Frank Spruill
219	Adams, Lionel Price	246	Alexander, Marion Romaine, Sr.
937	Adler, Christopher Edward		
384	Adler, Richard	1528	Alexander, Mary Elizabeth Perry
1516	Adler, Robert Sanford		
1239	Adler, Susan Emily	1435	Alexander, Renee Jacqueline
1655	Agarwal, Maneesha		
1482	Ahdieh, Omid	267	Alexander, Thomas Willis
974	Ahlport, Kathryn Newsome Campbell	247	Allen, Arch Turner
		1492	Allen, Arch Turner, III

689	Bass, E. Warner	1603	Beyle, Thad Lewis
586	Bass, Eddie Covington	1129	Bianchi, Robert John
1454	Batada, Ameena	1206	Biddell, Adrian John
1344	Bates, Tracey Marie	1036	Biddle, Ann Kellogg (*see*
	(*see* Leone)		Barker)
712	Battle, Charles Henry, Jr.	674	Bilbro, Robert Hodges
1423	Battle, George Edward, III	1080	Bilionis, Louis Dean
42	Battle, Kemp Davis	1397	Billing, John English
908	Batts, Valerie Alayne	498	Bilpuch, Edward George
1524	Baugh, Cindy Jo Werley	1391	Bingham, Natalie Dawn
1409	Baumann, Carl Christopher		Morgado
1193	Baxter, Edith Maria	342	Bishop, Donald Edwin
717	Bayer, Jeffrey Joshua	803	Bishop, E. Liston, III
1324	Beasley, Jody Keith	619	Bishop, Wayne Staton
594	Beatty, James Tully	393	Bishopric, Karl, Jr.
770	Beaver, Jeffrey Windsor	1370	Bissette, Winston Louis, III
1174	Beeson, Anne Milton	1128	Black, James Frederick
	(*see* Royalty)	431	Black, Kenneth, Jr.
1143	Beeson, Donald Eugene	659	Black, Stanley Warren, III
1253	Bell, Asa Lee, Jr.	1646	Black, Tiffany Mia
1611	Bell, Corey L.	1158	Blackburn, Frances Lucille
529	Bell, James Andrew	956	Blackburn, George
833	Bello, Thomas Michael		Templeton, II
920	Bellows, Amelia Helene	760	Blackwell, Hugh Allen
	(*see* Gleeson)	1321	Blanks, Tonya Robertina
397	Benbow, Charles Frank		(*see* Perry)
379	Bennett, Bert Lester, Jr.	1111	Bledsoe, Louis Adams, III
1245	Bennett, Herman Lee	1652	Blue, Rachel Teneil
1373	Benton, James Claude	1567	Bly, Donald André
1683	Benton, Kimberley Layne	1086	Boatwright, Ronald Gail
1119	Bergmann, Gale Marjorie	227	Bobbit, Joseph Rosser, Jr.
	Osborne	144	Bobbit, William Haywood
1242	Berney, Philip Edward	617	Boissavit, Jean Pierre
1102	Bernholz, Dorothy	1280	Bolch, Suzanne Elisabeth
	Cochrane	1303	Bolish, Nancy L.
468	Berryhill, Walter Reece	304	Bond, Niles Woodbridge
310	Bershak, Andrew A.	1248	Bondurant, Stuart
1689	Bethea, April Denise		Osborne, Jr.
1104	Betts, Doris Waugh	1139	Bondurant, Ward Scott

545	Creasy, Thomas Claiborne, Jr.	1717	Davis, Erin Nicole
		1390	Davis, Hubert Ira, Jr.
1215	Creech, David Capps, Jr.	266	Davis, J. Holmes, Jr.
327	Creedy, John Alan	334	Davis, James Evans
1522	Crisp, Charles Michael	390	Davis, James Rowlette
404	Crisp, William Thomas	221	Davis, John Conrad
204	Crissman, Walter E.	399	Davis, John Owen
895	Crittenton, Susan Anne Case	923	Davis, Joyce Leigh
		1022	Davis, Walter Paul
427	Crone, Ernest George	1103	Davis, Walter Royal
685	Cronenberg, Allen Thomson, Jr.	814	Dawson, Raymond Howard
		793	Day, Kenneth Coyner
50	Crosswell, James Earle	476	Daye, Anies Raphael, Jr.
1343	Crum, Catherine Claire	1276	Daye, Charles E.
640	Cummings, John Balentine	1108	Dean, Marcia Louise (*see* Onieal)
1167	Cumpsty, J. Michael		
825	Cunningham, Bruce Tracy, Jr.	530	Dear, Walter Moore, II
		575	Dearman, Henry Hursell
1451	Cunningham, James Calvin, III	447	Dedmond, Jesse Henry
		1607	Dees, Matthew Brent
1551	Cunningham, Nikolaus Ralf	62	Dees, William Archie
600	Cunningham, Robert Joseph	337	Dees, William Archie, Jr.
1698	Curtis, Jonathan Edward	1631	DeFriese, Gordon H.
1448	Dalal, Nilufer (*see* Loy)	1363	Deifell, Anthony Stuart
27	D'Alemberte, James Herring	691	Dellinger, Walter Estes, III
		127	DeRossett, Robert Cowan
271	Dameron, Emerson Penn	1472	Dervin, John Elliot
1194	D'Amico, Joseph Allen	1602	DeSaix, Jean Swaim
386	Damtoft, Walter Atkinson	1134	Detmer, William Matthew
277	Daniel, E. Clifton, Jr.	1172	DeVine, Mary Patricia
610	Daniels, Jonathan Worth	1078	DeVine, Stephen Ward
901	Daniels, Walter Etheridge	184	Deyton, John Wesley
808	Darrah, William Charles	827	Dibbert, Douglas Steven
1656	Daum, Jennifer Ann	743	Dickson, Paul, III
1428	Davidson, James	835	Didow, Nicholas Michael, Jr.
1458	Davidson, Stefanie Lynn	790	Dietz, John Edwin, II
257	Davis, Archibald K.	1351	DiGiano, Christopher John
710	Davis, Archie H.	1518	Dilg, Helen Lane

658	Farris, Ray Simpson, Jr.	655	Foushee, Roger Babson
1608	Fawcett, Anne Elizabeth (*see* Krishnan)	1375	Fox, Ulrich Alexander
		664	Frankfort, Hans R. E.
1580	Fay, Zachary Edling	832	Freeman, Franklin
1356	Featherstone, Gerald Lynn		Edward, Jr.
133	Feimster, Walter Connor, Jr.	749	Freeman, J. Lindsay
414	Fenhagen, F. Weston	609	Freeman, James Alexander
1729	Ferrell, Joseph S.	902	Freeman, Katherine Lynn
1690	Ferris, Frances Anne		Lloyd
687	Fetner, L. Jackson, II	69	Freeman, Robert Alexander
451	Fetzer, Robert Allison	1399	Friday, Ida Howell
94	Field, Bascom Lee	445	Friday, William Clyde
787	Findlay, William Allan	1338	Frye, Lisa Lanette (*see*
1520	Fischer, Alison Leigh		Garrison)
1159	Fischer, Anne Crowe	653	Fulk, Robert Vernon, Jr.
8	Fisher, William	182	Fuller, Henry Reasoner
400	Fitch, John S., Sr.	95	Fuller, Walter Pliny
598	Fitz-simons, Foster	724	Fullwood, James Roy
1682	Fjellstedt, Anders Paul	416	Fulton, Charles Lester
415	Flagler, Frederick James, Jr.	1539	Fulton, Shana LaVerne
1709	Flanagan, Shalane Grace	634	Furtado, Donald Atlas
566	Fleishman, Joel Lawrence	1101	Fuse-Hall, Rosalind Runae
1612	Florance, Meredith Grace	481	Fussell, Theodore James
1033	Floyd, Elson Sylvester	1670	Futrelle, G. Linwood, Jr.
705	Floyd, Joseph Summers, Jr.	232	Galland, Harry J.
930	Fogler, Murray Jules	363	Gambill, Ira Samuel
64	Folger, Alonzo Dillard	1141	Gardiner, Charles L.
1487	Foote, Shelby Dade	229	Gardner, Oliver Max
1030	Ford, Phil Jackson, Jr.	472	Gardner, Oliver Max, Jr.
406	Ford, Richard Bramley	288	Gardner, Ralph Webb
1027	Fordham, Christopher C., III	55	Garrett, Cecil Clark
198	Fordham, Jefferson B.	1338	Garrison, Lisa Lanette Frye
35	Fore, James Albert, Jr.	863	Gary, Richard David
561	Forester, J. Gordon, Jr.	822	Gaskin, James Reubin
1404	Forte, Stormie Denise	335	Gatton, T. Harry
1588	Fortune-Greeley, Hannah Cain	690	Gaulden, James Carlos, Jr.
		1301	Gebauer, Wendy Sue (*see* Palladino)
1320	Fountain, David Burton		
1235	Fountain, Edwin Louis	1298	Geer, Carol Parks

736	Geer, William Monroe	1559	Grano, Megan Elizabeth
958	George, Betty Glenn	145	Grant, Daniel Lindsey
1216	Germain, Suzanne Cobb	644	Gray, Charles Dowd, III
474	Gibson, Charles Robert	1092	Gray, Deborah Charleen
763	Gibson, Jonathan Carl	864	Gray, Frederick
1565	Gieseke, Amy Jo Scruggs		Pendleton, III
700	Gil, Frederico Guillermo	231	Gray, Gordon
1286	Gilbert, Durral Ray	1523	Gray, Kimberly Joy (*see*
1533	Gilmartin, Eamon Francis		Morgan)
332	Gilmore, Voit	218	Gray, R. McDonald
920	Gleeson, Amelia Helene	340	Green, Allen Jones
	Bellows	612	Green, Paul Eliot
205	Glenn, John Frazier, Jr.	1125	Greenberg, Bernard George
573	Gnanadesikan, Ramanathan	810	Greene, K. Edward
626	Godwin, Herman Allen, Jr.	235	Greene, Ralph Cordell
632	Goldsmith, Albert Lewis, Jr.	1049	Greenspan, Laura Leigh
1491	Goldstein, Burton		Scism
	Benjamin, Jr.	870	Griffin, William Barden
1394	Gonenne, Christy Lynn Pons	642	Grigg, David Lee
1379	Gooder, Harry	973	Grimsley, Jimmy Wayne
823	Gooding, Carnie Clayton, Jr.	824	Groome, Malcolm Murray
134	Gooding, Nathan Green	527	Gross, Edward Bailey
1710	Goodman, Carrie Elizabeth	1597	Grossman, Glenn Eric
244	Goodridge, Noah	1336	Guettel, Alexander Burton
461	Gordon, Richard Edmund	670	Gump, Louis Haynes
11	Gordon, William Jones	38	Gunter, Herbert Brown
525	Gorham, Robert D., Jr.	546	Gurley, Walter Dallas, Jr.
1471	Gourdet, Nicolas Patrice	942	Gustaveson, Norman
1408	Gowda, Deepthiman		Francis
	Krishne	1673	Guterman, Lydia Harris
1499	Gragg, Heralda Mavis	1541	Guthridge, William Wallace
B	Graham, Edward Kidder	478	Gwynn, James Minor
40	Graham, Frank Porter	173	Gwynn, William Wardlaw
9	Graham, Neill Ray	801	Haber, John Lawrence
759	Graham, William Albert, Jr.	201	Hackney, Bunn W., Jr.
568	Graham, William Edgar, Jr.	1398	Hadzija, Boka Wesley
1619	Graham-Bailey, Malika	898	Haigwood, Nancy Logan
	Josina Helena	683	Hall, Michael David

852	Hall, Peter Welles	457	Harrison, William Sherman, Jr.
597	Hallford, Edward Ulysses, Jr.	679	Harriss, William Graham
1096	Halpern, Linda Marie Cabe	1118	Harry, Randolph Herman
1196	Halpern, Lucia Veronica	1265	Hart, Todd Christopher
240	Hamer, Edward Ryan	176	Hartsell, Earle Horace
52	Hamilton, Oscar Alexander	1505	Harty, Justin Jerel
1412	Hamm, Mia Margaret	1650	Harvey, Marcus Donté
1536	Hammack, Scott Michael	366	Harward, Vernon Judson, Jr.
297	Hammer, Philip Gibbon	1661	Hashagen, Frederick William, III
374	Hammond, G. Denman		
177	Hampton, George Coggin, Jr.	1252	Hassel, Bryan Christopher
		1270	Hassel, Emily Urquhart Ayscue
952	Hancock, R. Darrell	1579	Hatchell, Sylvia R.
726	Hancock, William Geremain, Jr.	1307	Hathaway, Keith Stuart, Jr.
66	Hanes, Robert March	813	Hawfield, W. Benjamine, Jr.
528	Haney, James Lawton, Jr.	185	Hawkins, James E.
437	Hanft, Frank William	1410	Hawkins, William Lee, Jr.
929	Hardee, Sandra Grace	1529	Hawthorne, Lacey Adele (see Leegwater)
1462	Hardin, Paul		
1053	Hardison, Dee	1486	Hayes, David Neil
1037	Hardy, Lonza Calvin, Jr.	361	Hayes, George Lewis
1000	Hardy, Martha Nell Zant	706	Hays, W. Arthur, Jr.
677	Hargrove, Wade Hampton, Jr.	4	Haywood, Alfred Williams, Jr.
752	Harmon, John Matney	19	Haywood, Hubert Benbury
1368	Harmon, Quaker Elizabeth Kappel	1309	Haywood, Kenneth Clarke
		1449	Headrick, Nathan Paul
5	Harper, Ralph Moore	318	Heard, G. Alexander
242	Harper, William Lacy, Sr.	1197	Heaton, Mary Margaret Jones
146	Harrell, Beemer Clifford		
703	Harrington, Anthony Stephen	1538	Hedt, Bethany Lynn
		1554	Heinke, Nicholas Peter
1519	Harris, Charles Joseph	516	Henderson, Archibald
1715	Harris, Katherine Jennifer	233	Henderson, John Middleton
369	Harris, Louis	1140	Henderson, Mary Josephine (see Bowman)
1728	Harris, Trudier		
455	Harris, W. Page, Jr.	1077	Heneghan, Daniel Francis

320	Hudson, Henry Edward	1452	Jaworsky, Tommy Joe, II
77	Huffman, Robert Obediah	429	Jefferies, Raymond
996	Huggins, L. Victor		Lewis, Jr.
31	Hughes, Harvey Hatcher	806	Jeffress, Charles Neville
816	Hull, Floyd Carol, III	1251	Jenkins, Mary Campbell
1466	Hultquist, Katherine Grace	489	Jenrette, Richard Hampton
948	Humphries, C. Thomas	1548	Jernigan, David Wayne
408	Hunt, Douglass	1121	Jessiman, Thomas Antony
1177	Hunt, James Baxter, Jr.	1009	Johnson, Allen Herbert, III
1625	Hunter, Kathleen R.	1380	Johnson, Audreye E.
758	Hunter, Robert Carl	1624	Johnson, Eric David
630	Huntington, Charles	1600	Johnson, James H., Jr.
	Riddell, Sr.	110	Johnson, John Gray
1283	Hurst, Patricia Lyn	1627	Johnson, John Hiram, III
1723	Hurwitz, Amy Samara	1182	Johnson, Keith Harrison
949	Husted, Joseph Spencer	656	Johnson, M. Glen
54	Hyman, Orren William	960	Johnson, Michael Richard
1510	Ibrahim, Michel A.	1457	Johnson, Michelle Lesley
688	Imes, William Carl	1115	Johnson, Robert Edward
757	Ingram, George Mason, IV	287	Johnson, Thor Martin
750	Ingram, John Carter	469	Johnston, Charles Louis, Jr.
1716	Iravani, Heide Motaghi	1271	Johnston, James Thornhill
1178	Irvine, Edward Claywell	44	Johnston, John Thomas
695	Irvine, James Nelson	1438	Johnston, Nicholas Simon
1059	Isaacs, Hanan Mayer		MacPherson
947	Israel, Mae Helen	210	Johnston, Samuel Nash
325	Ivey, Alfred Guy	1221	Johnston, Sarah Urban
1641	Ivey, Laura A.	191	Jonas, Charles Raper, Sr.
1427	Jablonski, Kimberly Erin	1056	Jones, Gary Durward
	McCutcheon	882	Jones, Harry Louis
1476	Jackson, George Lee	1224	Jones, Houston G.
1256	Jackson, Odessa Palmer	625	Jones, Jesse Weimar
156	Jacobi, David Beuthner	1197	Jones, Mary Margaret (*see*
7	Jacocks, William Picard		Heaton)
953	Jacokes, Paul Douglas	1258	Jones, Raymond Clifton
30	James, James Burton	1617	Jones, Rebecca Taylor Lea
935	James, Reid Clain	818	Jones, Robert Brooke
1527	Jamison, Antawn Cortez	1048	Jones, William Bain, Jr.

58	Jones, William Henry
549	Jordan, L. Russell
1186	Jordan, Michael Jeffrey
564	Jordan, Ralph Martin, Jr.
319	Jordan, William Stone, Jr.
344	Joslin, William
858	Jost, Peter Hafner
138	Joyner, Claude R.
456	Joyner, Edward Grey, Jr.
322	Joyner, James McMurray
49	Joyner, James Noah
464	Justice, Charles
359	Kanter, Edward Lewis
1068	Kapp, M. Keith
1368	Kappel, Quaker Elizabeth (*see* Harmon)
1345	Karcher, Timothy Quaid
886	Karl, George Matthew
383	Karres, Steve Matthew
1287	Kashani-Sabet, Firoozeh
848	Kassens, William Diedrich, Jr.
912	Kastleman, Kenneth Mayer
582	Katzenstein, Charles J., Jr.
588	Kearns, Thomas Francis, Jr.
1136	Keeshan, Nancy Kay
1189	Keesler, David Culver
1212	Kelley, Katharine Wilkes
1113	Kelley, Pamela Sue
438	Kelly, J. Patrick
1100	Kelly, John Brendan
1684	Kelly, Leia Michelle
1331	Kenan, Thomas Stephen, III
1064	Kendall, Robert John
914	Kennedy, Daniel
1238	Kennedy, John Lacy, Jr.
147	Kerr, John Hosea, Jr.
1645	Kertesz, Johanna Susan

775	Kiel, David Harris
1494	Kilbourne, James Walter, Jr.
385	Kilpatrick, John Thomas, Jr.
345	Kimball, Clyde Gates
1157	Kimball, William Hugo
1285	Kimmelman, Robin P.
1444	King, Bradley Ross
1142	King, Caleb Kimball
1222	King, Dean Howard
741	King, Malvern Francis, Jr.
449	Kirkland, John Alvin
458	Kirkland, Robert Edward, Jr.
638	Kirkman, A. Larkin
990	Kirkman, Roger Norman
1696	Kirkpatrick, Robert Galloway, Jr.
1700	Kistin, Elizabeth James
1445	Kitchens, Rupa Virupaksha Kothandapani
1065	Klein, Martha Elizabeth Sellers
1697	Kleinman, Sherryl
1623	Kleysteuber, William Rudolph, IV
348	Kline, Charles Robert
1484	Koonce, Thomas Fredrick
1445	Kothandapani, Rupa Virupaksha (*see* Kitchens)
581	Kraar, Louis
1501	Kraft, Katherine Lorraine
1312	Krebs, Thomas Robert
786	Krichbaum, George West, Jr.
1608	Krishnan, Anne Elizabeth Fawcett
1035	Kummel, Charles Maxwell
548	Kuralt, Charles Bishop
206	Kyser, James Kay

1294 Lackey, Victoria Kathleen Marjorie Donovan
1017 LaGarde, Thomas Joseph
957 Lake, Marsha Benton Mann
1695 Lam, William C.
1012 Lamb, Bradley Robert
574 Lambeth, Thomas Willis
514 Lamm, James Louis DeLay
452 Landreth, Monroe Mitchell
1633 Lane, Mary Turner
1701 Langberg, Jason Brett
1341 Langman, James Elliott
838 Langstroth, Leland Alfred
403a Lanier, Edwin Sidney
1677 Lanier, Gregory Ryan
1133 Lanier, Jennifer Anne
1209 Lankard, Bryce Aaron
766 Lapkin, David Theodore
1349 Largess, Stephen Luke
1171 Latham, Vicki LeGrand
1340 Latimer, Lee Winston (*see* Loughran)
850 LaTour, Stephen Alexis
1712 Laughlin, Jonas Blaine
697 Lawler, Michael Henry
911 Layton, Bruce David
1497 Le, Trinh Thi
1617 Lea, Rebecca Taylor (*see* Jones)
83 Leach, Oscar
463 Leary, Joseph Clarence, Jr.
1107 Leaver, Evelyn Ruth (*see* Marinshaw)
660 Leavitt, Sturgis Elleno
966 Lee, Howard Nathaniel
784 Lee, Maurice W.
1529 Leegwater, Lacey Adele Hawthorne

1544 LeFebvre, Donna Harrison
1233 Lefler, Elizabeth Ashley (*see* Wilson)
423 Lefler, Hugh Talmage
1116 Leight, Margaret Graham
1665 Leloudis, James Linwood, II
1376 Lennard, Sean
1026 Lensing, George, Jr.
501 Leonard, Colvin Theodore, Jr.
834 Leonard, J. Rich
1344 Leone, Tracey Marie Bates
633 LeRoy, E. Carwile
1574 Leuchtenburg, William E.
1175 Leutze, James R.
917 Levin, Richard Ivor
1461 Levine, Allison Jane Taylor
651 Levy, Edwin
349 Lewis, Wellington H.
1339 Lewis, William David Brien
152 Liipfert, Benjamin Bailey
537 Likins, Paul Ross
117 Lindau, Alfred Milton
980 Lindsay, Susan Battige
139 Lindsey, Edwin Samuel
189 Lineberger, Henry Abel
199 Lineberger, J. Harold
121 Linker, Joe Burton
103 Linn, Thomas Calvin
1334 Little, C. Crowell
754 Little, James David
1593 Little, Joseph Alexander
1262 Little, Walter Leake Parsons
1273 Little, William Frederick
1439 Liu, David Wei
1070 Livermore, Ann Mario Martinelli
170 Llewellyn, Clement Manly

637 Mason, Wilton Elman, Jr.
1176 Massey, Charles Knox, Sr.
972 Mathews, Robert
    Cabeen H., III
1480 Matsen, Susanna Lovell
1034 Mattox, Nancy Ann
1246 Mauer, Charles E.
762 Maupin, Armistead
    Jones, Jr.
237 Maus, James Reginald
702 Mayer, Henry
645 Mayo, John Blount, Jr.
1071 Mayo, Thomas Bolton, III
883 McAdams, Katherine Vaden
    Carlton
959 McAllaster, Carolyn
294 McCachren, James Roland
746 McCallie, S. Wyatt
836 McCauley, Donald
    Frederick, Jr.
1295 McClellan, Lucy Dell (see
    Steiner)
1626 McClure, Christopher
    Douglas
263 McClure, David Craig
1526 McCollum, Marc Stewart
1047 McConnell, Joseph Moore
1190 McCoy, David Timothy
440 McCoy, Donald Whitfield
1599 McCoy, William Octavius
1427 McCutcheon, Kimberly Erin
    (see Jablonski)
719 McDevitt, Larry Stephen
164 McDonald, Angus Morris
1525 McDonald, Raegan E. (see
    Mosley)
1308 McDonnell, Pamela Jean
    (see Perry)

841 McDowell, John Patrick, III
1556 McDuffie, Janora Ann
106 McDuffie, Roger Atkinson
1162 McElhaney, Jeffrey James
338 McGaughey, Carroll
    Bradford, Jr.
857 McGaughey, Harry Stephen
165 McGee, Alan Marshall
1563 McGee, Janey Roxanna
    Phelps
1663 McGhee, Jasmine Spring
731 McGinty, Park
312 McGlinn, Frank C. P.
1621 McGlone, Emilie Pamela
607 McGuire, Frank J.
854 McGuire, Joseph Pinckney
499 McIntyre, James Herbert
200 McIver, Herman Martin
830 McKeagney, Robert B., Jr.
306 McKee, Donald Kennedy
265 McKee, William Wakefield
18 McLean, Frank
826 McLean, Jack Linden, Jr.
157 McLean, Joseph Altira
418 McLendon, Lennox Polk, Jr.
936 McLendon, Mae Belle
554 McLendon, William
    Woodard
540 McLeod, George Holliday
535 McLeod, James Carlisle, Jr.
1672 McManus, Julie Cecelia
918 McMillan, James Bryan, Sr.
809 McMurray, John William
1202 McNamara, Mary Elizabeth
    Evans
409 McNeely, William Fennell
1478 McNerney, Katherine Seton

797 Mosteller, Robert Paul
1585 Mulder, Erin Elizabeth Cooper
1289 Mulvey, Kathryn Louise
560 Muntzing, L. Manning
420 Murchison, Wallace Carmichael
495 Murphy, Richard James F.
190 Murphy, Spencer
994 Murray, Alan Stewart
773 Myer, C. Randolph, III
1605 Myers, Devon Ann
542 Myers, Kenneth M.
1230 Myers, Vikki Jaye Barrett
1707 Nagaraj, Sunil S.
96 Nance, Ophir Carmal
162 Nash, Marion W.
53 Nash, Thomas Palmer
884 Nash, Thomas Palmer, IV
1503 Nathan, Mohan
728 Neely, Charles Batcheller, Jr.
523 Neill, Rolfe
1637 Newman, Sundarkia Shanta (see Hill)
97 Newsome, Albert Ray
394 Newsome, James Frederick
881 Nicholson, Britain Walton
1571 Nieman, Jeffrey Larkin
1148 Norberg, Scott Fredrik
1724 Nussbaum, Abraham M.
531 Oberdorfer, Eugene, II
509 Odum, Howard Washington
1214 Ofseyer, Jeremy Joshua
868 Oglesby, Mary Norris Preyer
1151 Okun, Daniel Alexander
1447 Oliver, George Mason
1470 Oliver, Pamela Kaye Alston

739 Oliver, R. Timothy
1234 Olson, Janet Anne (see Roberts)
435 O'Neall, John Schofield, Jr.
274 O'Neil, John Tettemer
1108 Onieal, Marcia Louise Dean
585 Oppenheimer, Jerry L.
1135 Orr, Elizabeth Corinne Brady
1119 Osborne, Gail Marjorie (see Bergmann)
372 Osborne, Henry Plant, Jr.
1392 Ose, Erik Dexter
747 O'Toole, Dennis Theodore
1032 Owens, Raymond Eugene, Jr.
1191 Owens, Richard David
855 Padrick, Joseph Michael
1693 Page, Branson Halsted
1301 Palladino, Wendy Sue Gebauer
1249 Palmer, Colin A.
1720 Panjabi, Rajesh Ramesh
1521 Papon, Lucienne Claire
197 Parker, Henry N.
939 Parker, John A.
180 Parker, John Johnston
316 Parker, John Johnston, Jr.
105 Parker, John Merrell
1039 Parker, Kathleen Ann
1183 Parker, Paul Gray
1093 Parker, Sharon Lee
1044 Parks, Sheri LaDeanne
1549 Parlow, Cynthia Marie
1050 Parmelee, William Douglas
873 Parnell, Samuel Michael
1504 Parrish, Erin G. (see Reade)
273 Parsley, Henry Nutt, Sr.

296	Pool, Rufus Adolphus
1300	Poole, Darrin Maurice
159	Porter, Garland Burns
1052	Porter, Gregory Douglas
1031	Porter, Joni Ann Peters
1066	Porterfield, William David
591	Poteat, William H.
875	Potter, Deborah Ann
552	Potter, Edward Lex
1659	Potter, Mary Elizabeth
308	Potts, Ramsay D.
1691	Powell, Deone Demetris
135	Powell, John William Gordon
761	Powell, Robert Stone, Jr.
999	Powell, William Stevens
579	Powledge, Fred
519	Pregnall, William S.
1649	Presler, Henrietta Heiss
1420	Presler, Myles O'Hara
1553	Presnell, Sabrina Kathleen (see Rockoff)
876	Previs, Stephen Richard
992	Preyer, Jane Bethell
866	Preyer, L. Richardson
868	Preyer, Mary Norris (see Oglesby)
668	Price, David Eugene
471	Pritchard, William Grady, Jr.
228	Pritchett, Hoyt Baker
84	Pritchett, James Turner
1228	Pritchett, Mebane Moore
556	Pruitt, Kenneth Melvin
1606	Pruitt, Terry Wayne
927	Pullen, Emma Eliza
422	Pully, Morris Wiley
1091	Pulver, Robin Gilles
178	Purser, John R., Jr.

905	Putnam, David Lawrence
1610	Quarles, Ann Elizabeth
892	Queen, Anne Ellen
613	Quigg, Joseph Francis
313	Rabb, Stuart White, Jr.
589	Ragsdale, George Robinson
343	Ralston, George Francis
113	Ramsay, James Graham
253	Ramsay, Kerr Craige
1546	Rand, Anthony Eden
290	Rand, Hubert Hinton
114	Rand, Oliver Gray
36	Rand, Oscar Ripley
202	Raney, R. Beverly, Sr.
720	Range, Peter Ross
90	Rankin, Edgar Ralph
682	Rash, J. Dennis
323	Read, Nicholas Cabell
1504	Reade, Erin G. Parrish
1704	Reddick, Catherine Anne
1430	Reed, John Shelton, Jr.
45	Reeves, Jeremiah Bascom
950	Reeves, Nancy Ruth (see Mansfield)
1016	Reid, John Coleman
879	Reid, Lawrence Alan
1537	Reid, Tracy Lashawn
1436	Reinglass, Carolyn Renee
1317	Reist, Adam Aston
1591	Rentas, Lerissa Yvette
1385	Rentz, Meridith Leigh
940	Renwick, H. Bently
1231	Reynolds, Kimberly Sue
526	Rezutto, Thomas Anthony, Jr.
1123	Richardson, Richard J.
1014	Richardson, William Odum
339	Richter, Horace

1200 Schoultz, Lars Gustav
1274 Schroeder, Frederic W., Jr.
969 Schwartz, Joel Joseph
1406 Schwartz, Rona Adele
1614 Schwartz-Barcott, Rye M.
(*see* Barcott)
1049 Scism, Laura Leigh (*see*
Greenspan)
1642 Scott, Carmen Laverne
641 Scott, James Martin
730 Scott, Ralph Henderson
502 Scroggs, Robin Jerome
1565 Scruggs, Amy Jo (*see*
Gieseke)
629 Scurlock, David Caesar, Jr.
1362 Seagrave, Sharon Renee
Couch
1062 Segal, Alethea Gail
460 Seixas, E. Victor, Jr.
1065 Sellers, Martha Elizabeth
(*see* Klein)
354 Severin, Paul Vincent, Sr.
1110 Seymour, Frances Jane
524 Seymour, Thaddeus
983 Shackelford, Susan Patricia
187 Shackell, Aubrey Earle
1105 Shadroui, George Phillip
704 Shaffer, Charles Milton, Jr.
1124 Shaffer, Charles Milton, Sr.
314 Shaffner, Louis Des
1443 Shah, Sneha Champak (*see*
Coltrane)
1003 Sharp, Susie Marshall
1138 Sharpe, Amy Marie
1498 Shastri, Kirti Ann
148 Shaw, John Duncan
802 Shedd, Joseph Blake
740 Shelburne, John Daniel
1413 Shelburne, Mark Howard

1632 Sheldon, George Frank
1669 Shelton, Karen C.
149 Shepard, Fredrick Carlyle
1450 Shepherd, Rebecah Caroline
Moore
1028 Sheps, Cecil G.
443 Sherrill, Basil Lamar
1015 Shiffman, Lili Anna (*see*
Arkin)
991 Shirley, Lawrence
Elman, Jr.
1166 Shiver, Gerrie Michelle (*see*
Wysinger)
270 Shoemaker, Donald C.
910 Shore, Martha Elizabeth
(*see* Edwards)
346 Shuford, William Melvin
513 Shupine, Jerry Monroe
1019 Shuping, Sallie Murrill (*see*
Russell)
1469 Sides, John Michael
977 Simonton, Charles
Alison, III
1595 Simpson, Dana Edward
1377 Sipress, Joel Michael
1150 Sitterson, J. Carlyle
1687 Slain, Jonathan Philip
941 Slifkin, Miriam Kresses
26 Sloan, Henry Lee
725 Sloane, Joseph C.
251 Slusser, Frank Williard
1207 Smith, Albertina Denise (*see*
Smith-Banks)
1020 Smith, Barry Lynn
167 Smith, Calvin Upshur
1114 Smith, Carolyn Moore
1456 Smith, Charlotte Daniele
(*see* Smith-Taylor)
805 Smith, Dean E.

315   Smith, J. McNeill, Jr.
1255 Smith, Kenneth
1699 Smith, Michael Rollan
631   Smith, Norman Barrett
714   Smith, Roger William
1426 Smith, Ruth Maxine Campbell
1419 Smith, Timothy Cornail
639   Smith, Wade Marvin
362   Smith, Wilburn Jackson, Jr.
1207 Smith-Banks, Albertina Denise
1456 Smith-Taylor, Charlotte Daniele
590   Sneden, John Aitken, Jr.
737   Sneed, Albert Lee, Jr.
889   Snider, William Davis
933   Snodgrass, William James
373   Snyder, Ben McClellan, III
305   Snyder, Jacob Elias
466   Sobel, David Elliott
1029 Sockwell, Samuel Thomas
517   Somerville, Paul N.
654   Spain, Jack Holland, Jr.
1431 Spangler, Clemmie Dixon, Jr.
723   Spearman, Robert W.
220   Spearman, Walter Smith
382   Spence, Robert Atwell, Sr.
484   Sper, Norman Leopold, Jr.
1676 Spillman, Amanda Danielle (*see* Stokes)
141   Spruill, Corydon Perry
1352 Spykerman, Virginia Jordan Mewborne
486   Stacy, Horace Edney, Jr.
32   Stacy, Walter Parker
851   Stallings, Joseph Henry
815   Stallings, W. Daniel

1046 Stamper, Robert Cecil, Jr.
648   Stanley, Raymond J. T.
1165 Staton, Lisa Anne (*see* Dyer)
1278 Steele, Henry Max
123   Steele, William T.
985   Steelman, Bennett Loftin
1418 Stegman, Michael Allen
1083 Steigerwald, William Richard
1295 Steiner, Lucy Dell McClellan
1372 Steiner, Michael Newport (*see* Ulku-Steiner)
928   Stephenson, William Elliott
1324 Stephenson, William Hermas
1639 Stepp, Jennifer Royce
522   Stevens, Edward Amos
783   Stevens, H. Hugh, Jr.
256   Stevens, Henry Leonidas, Jr.
887   Stevens, Richard Yates
1063 Stevenson, Karen Leslie
56   Stewart, Barney Cleveland
1393 Stewart, Matthew Dan
1   Stewart, Roach Sidney
1208 Stinneford, Mark Stephen
426   Stockton, Robert Gray, Sr.
1676 Stokes, Amanda Danielle Spillman
74   Stokes, Walter, Jr.
1463 Stone, Chuck S., Jr.
1417 Stone, Sonja Haynes
1575 Stout, Cheryl Barbour
78   Strange, Robert, Jr.
596   Strassler, Paul Gene
430   Strayhorn, Ralph Nichols, Jr.
1122 Strayhorn, Susan Elaine (*see* Barbour)
1437 Strickler, John Howard

85	Strong, George Vaughn	432	Taylor, William West
871	Strong, Jay Nelson	70	Teague, Claude Edward
377	Strowd, Roy Ervin	48	Teague, Dossey Battle
223	Strudwick, Shepperd	727	Temple, Gray, Jr.
976	Stuart, Catherine Janis Rosenthal	126	Tennent, Charles Galliard
		671	Tennille, Norton Fortune, Jr.
698	Stubbs, Trawick Hamilton, Jr.	1702	Tepper, Matthew Samuel
		1310	Tepper, Steven Jay
1180	Stumpf, Andrea Emily	1074	Terrell, Thomas Eugene, Jr.
989	Sugar, Harriet Sue	1679	Terry, Samantha Elizabeth
286	Sugarman, Joseph J.	982	Thomas, Gary Watson
1184	Sullivan, Timothy Patrick	1552	Thomas, Kevin Clarence
693	Sullivan, William Ross	1411	Thomas, Michelle Lisa
534	Sully, Thomas Alfred	1007	Thomas, Nova Rebecca
1674	Sura, Siddharth Piyush	744	Thomas, W. Neil, III
584	Sutton, Edward Wike	47	Thomas, William George
1001	Swalin, Benjamin Franklin	520	Thomason, Robert Hume
1644	Swinson, Davene DaShawn	60	Thompson, Gordon Wesley
1277	Swofford, John Douglas	395	Thompson, W. Reid
441	Szafaryn, Leonard Adolph	1508	Thornburg, Ryan Michael
487	Talley, Banks Cooper, Jr.	1647	Thornton, David Dontay
1058	Talmadge, Linda Louise Love	1315	Thorp, Clay Bernardin
		1664	Thorp, Herbert Holden
1507	Tan, Daniel Henry	370	Thorp, John Daniel
59	Tanner, Kenneth Spencer	183	Thorpe, Richard Young
442	Tate, William Knox, Sr.	1314	Thurtle, Laurie Anne Winkler
1299	Taubman, Andrew Bennett		
125	Tayloe, John Cotten	46	Tillett, Charles Walter
1461	Taylor, Allison Jane (see Levine)	358	Tillett, Charles Walter, Jr.
		29	Tillett, Duncan Patterson
1495	Taylor, Chandra Terice	63	Tillett, John
673	Taylor, George V.	72	Tillett, William Smith
295	Taylor, Herbert Hamilton, Jr.	615	Tillman, C. Hunter
		1229	Tillman, Otis Edward, Jr.
364	Taylor, Isaac M.	555	Tillman, Rollie, Jr.
353	Taylor, Nelson Ferebee	1008	Tindall, Bruce McGarrity
559	Taylor, Raymond Mason	1024	Toben, Boyd Stephen
551	Taylor, Tyre Crumpler	1181	Tomlinson, Tresa Suzette Brown
89	Taylor, Walter Frank		

269	Weathers, Virgil Stowe	844	Wicker, Thomas Grey
299	Weaver, Frederick Henry	402	Wideman, Frank James, Jr.
565	Webb, R. Beverly	71	Wiggins, Archibald Lee
87	Webster, Felix Litaker		Manning
387	Webster, W. Terrell, Jr.	967	Wiggins, Edith Mayfield
258	Weeks, O. Haywood, Sr.	347	Wiggins, Lee M.
1464	Wegner, Judith Welch	211	Wilkins, Robert Wallace
1084	Weir, Heather Hope Helen	1376	Wilkinson, Christopher
	(*see* Boneparth)		Sean (*see* Lennard)
1095	Weiss, Jennifer	733	Willard, Kenneth
356	Welborn, Joseph Alson		Henderson
577	Wells, Samuel Fogle, Jr.	1654	Willett, Kristen Suzanne
774	Welt, Louis Gordon	862	Williams, Arthur Shelden
1524	Werley, Cindy Jo (*see*	160	Williams, C. J.
	Baugh)	1643	Williams, Caroline Austin
1653	Werry, Scott Samuel		Alexander
1703	West, Haley Elizabeth	1023	Williams, David Cratis
946	West, Thomas Roswell	A	Williams, Henry Horace
1562	Whaley, Amy Lorene	238	Williams, James William
1714	Wheeler, Ashton Lee	1254	Williams, John Wesley, II
692	Wheeler, Grant Walton	1388	Williams, Kimberly Ann (*see*
675	Wheless, Dwight Hernard		Moore)
1467	Wherry, Frederick	926	Williams, Marcus Whitman
	Fitzgerald	1572	Williams, Mary Katherine
669	Whichard, Willis Padgett		(*see* Roederer)
207	Whisnant, Manly Dowell	777	Williams, Michael Wayne
368	Whitaker, Frank Ridley, Jr.	1668	Williams, Richard Tyrone
622	Whitaker, John Clarke, Jr.	1203	Williams, Tommy Earl
142	White, Edwin Emerson	729	Williams, Willis Howard
401	White, Harvey O'Neal	1530	Williamson, Emily Lynn
1477	White, Katharine Faye	301	Williamson, Harry Webb
963	Whitefield, Clarence Earl	1421	Williamson, Matthew David
608	Whitelock, Harry Earl	925	Williamson, Pamela Anne
817	Whitfield, James Lawrence	1055	Williamson, Samuel R., Jr.
86	Whiting, Seymour Webster	1367	Williams-Tracy, Jeffrey Scott
1333	Whitted, Alexine A.	1675	Williford, Rebecca Susanne
1347	Whittier, Donald Andrews	302	Willingham, Francis
616	Whitty, John Christopher		Fries, Sr.

300	Willis, Benjamin Sheppard	1407	Wooten, Patrick Sloan
1515	Willis, Rachel A.	329	Worley, Richard Campbell
1233	Wilson, Elizabeth Ashley Lefler	17	Worth, Henry Venable
		262	Wright, Lenoir Chambers
494	Wilson, James Wood	921	Wright, Thomas Henry, III
1192	Wilson, John Bernhardt, Jr.	1187	Wulfhorst, Debra Lynn (*see* Cole)
603	Wilson, Louis Round		
652	Wilson, Mark King, III	1589	Wurth, Emily Louise
1236	Wilson, Michael Roscoe	1166	Wysinger, Gerrie Michelle Shiver
869	Wilson, Robert Reid		
21	Winborne, John Wallace	1708	Yang, Sendra
1314	Winkler, Laurie Ann (*see* Thurtle)	563	Yarborough, Charles Hill, Jr.
		248	Yarborough, William H., Jr.
41	Winslow, Francis Edward	485	Yates, Herbert Seawell
1117	Winston, James Horner, Jr.	39	Yelverton, William Elmer
67	Winston, Robert Watson, Jr.	1297	Yelverton, William Forrest, II
874	Witt, G. Evans		
434	Woestendiek, William J.	562	Yoder, Edwin Milton, Jr.
504	Wolf, William Thomas	1040	York, Maurice Clifton
51	Wolfe, Adolphus Harrison	128	York, William Marvin
143	Wolfe, Thomas Clayton	1638	Young, Justin Coleman
665	Womack, Nathan Anthony	569	Young, Robert Terry
1511	Woodard, Harold	169	Young, Victor Vernon
628	Woodard, Paul Lindsey	479	Young, William Frederick
492	Woodhouse, Edward James	1268	Zook, James Randolph, Jr.
98	Woollcott, Philip	1383	Zucker, Nancy Lee
14	Woollen, Charles Thomas		

Roster of Officers, 1904–2004

(table starts on following page)

Year	Jason	Hyparchos	Grammateus	Chrystopher
Spring 1904	Alfred Williams Haywood Jr.	Sidney Swain Robins	Albert Lyman Cox	Ralph Moore Harper
Fall 1904	Claiborn McDowell Carr	Newnan Alexander Townsend	Charles Thomas Woolen	Charles Carroll Barnhart
Spring 1905	Frank McLean	no record	Charles Thomas Woolen	no record
Fall 1905	Agnew Hunter Bahnson	Thomas Grier Miller	Robert Edward Calder	Frederick Mull Crawford
Spring 1906	Thomas Grier Miller	no record	Robert Edward Calder	Frederick Mull Crawford
1906–07	Henry Lee Sloan	Wiley Hassell Marion Pittman	James Herring D'Alemberte	Duncan Patterson Tillett
1907–08	Simon Rae Logan	no record	James Albert Fore Jr.	Herbert Brown Gunter
1908–09	Frank Porter Graham	Kemp Davis Battle	Francis Edward Winslow	Charles Walter Tillett
1909–10	Dossey Battle Teague	Adolphus Harrison Wolfe	Thomas Palmer Nash	James Noah Joyner
1910–11	Barney Cleveland Stewart	William Archibald Dees	Gordon Wesley Thompson	Kenneth Spencer Tanner
1911–12	Robert Alexander Freeman	Robert Watson Winston Jr.	Lawrence Nelson Morgan	Robert March Hanes
1912–13	Archibald Lee Manning Wiggins	William Smith Tillett	Douglass Le'Tell Rights	Walter Stokes Jr.
1913–14	John Scott Cansler	Seymour Webster Whiting	George Vaughan Strong	James Turner Pritchett
1914–15	Bascom Lee Field	no record	Walter Pliny Fuller	no record
1915–16	Francis Foster Bradshaw	Robert Burton House	Giles Mebane Long	Roy McRae Homewood
1916–17	Oliver Gray Rand	Herman Glenn Baity	William Tannahill Polk	James Graham Ramsay
1917–18	William Trabue Steele	Charles Holmes Herty Jr.	Joseph Burton Linker	Charles Galliard Tennent
Fall 1918	Theodore Edward Rondthaler	no record	William Clement Eaton	no record
Spring 1919	Jefferson Carney Bynum	no record	Robert Franklin Moseley	no record
1919–20	Edwin Samuel Lindsey	Claude Rueben Joyner	Nathan Mobley	Corydon Perry Spruill
Fall 1920	Daniel Lindsey Grant	William Haywood Bobbit	John Duncan Shaw	Beemer Clifford Harrell
Spring 1921	Daniel Lindsey Grant	William Haywood Bobbit	John Duncan Shaw	Frederick Carlyle Shepard
1921–22	Benjamin Bailey Lüpfert	Joseph Altira McLean	Luther James Phipps	George Watts Hill
1922–23	Allen Marshall McGee	Angus Morris McDonald	Victor Vernon Young	Julius Jennings Wade

Year	Jason	Hyparchos	Grammateus	Chrystopher
1923–24	no record	no record	no record	no record
1924–25	William Johnston Cocke	no record	no record	no record
1925–26	Jefferson Barnes Fordham	no record	Lawrence Eugene Watt	no record
1926–27	Bunn Washington Hackney Jr.	no record	no record	no record
1927–28	Robert Wallace Wilkins	no record	Edward Alexander Cameron	no record
1928–29	Robert McDonald Gray	no record	no record	no record
1929–30	Gordon Gray	no record	Harry Joseph Galland	no record
1930–31	Edward Ryan Hamer	no record	no record	no record
1931–32	Robert Mayne Albright	no record	no record	no record
1932–33	William Wakefield McKee	no record	no record	no record
1933–34	Bennett Harper Barnes	no record	no record	no record
1934–35	Franklin Pierce Abernethy Jr.	no record	no record	no record
1935–36	Thomas Moore Evins	no record	no record	no record
1936–37	Frederick Henry Weaver	no record	no record	no record
1937–38	Ramsay Douglas Potts	no record	no record	no record
1938–39	James McMurray Joyner	no record	no record	no record
1939–40	Edward Haywood Megson	no record	no record	no record
1940–41	William Archibald Dees Jr.	no record	no record	no record
1941–42	Nelson Ferebee Taylor	no record	no record	no record
1942–43	Vernon Judson Harward Jr.	no record	no record	no record
1943–44	John Mosely Robinson Jr.	no record	no record	no record
	George Denman Hammond			
	Robert Norton Burleigh			
1944–45	James Frederick (Turk) Newsome	no record	no record	no record

[207]

Year	Jason	Hyparchos	Grammateus	Chrystopher
1945–46	Edward Frankling Emack	Charles Fogle Vance Jr.	William Jennings Tripp	William Jennings Tripp
1946–47	Charles Fogle Vance Jr.	no record	Winston Broadfoot	Robert Gray Stockton Sr.
1947–48	Ralph Nichols Strayhorn Jr.	Charles Lester Fulton	Charles Frederic Warren	Robert Gray Stockton Sr.
1948–49	William Houston Miller	Wayne Brenengen	William Robert Coulter	Basil Lamar Sherill
1949–50	Jesse Henry Dedmond	Allard Kenneth Lowenstein	Harold Lee Andrews	William Donald Carmichael III
		Samuel Hays Magill		
1950–51	Edward Kuykendall Washington	John Lassiter Sanders	Charles Samuel Bartlett Jr.	James Minor Gwynn
1951–52	Edward George Bilpuch	John Lassiter Sanders	James Clarence Wallance	William Davis Cash
1952–53	Julian Dewey Mason Jr.	John Martin Schnorrenberg	Kenneth Houston Barton	Paul Noble Somerville
1953–54	Kenneth Lawing Penegar	Thaddeus Seymour	Rolfe Neill	James Lawton Haney Jr.
1954–55	Horace Edney Stacy Jr.	Walter Dallas Gurley Jr.	Lemuel Russell Jordan	Paul Ross Likins
1955–56	Thomas Claiborne Creasy Jr.	Lewis Manning Muntzing	Richard Berverly Raney Webb	Charles Hill Yarborough Jr.
1956–57	Thomas Claiborne Creasy Jr.	William Thomas Wolf	William Ray Long	Thomas Willis Lambeth
1957–58	Thomas Willis Lambeth	William Ray Long	John Aiken Sneden Jr.	Peter Joseph Brennan
1958–59	Raymond Mason Taylor	Paul Genen Strassler	Harvey Peck	John Clarke Whitaker Jr.
1959–60	Paul Gene Strassler	Norman Barrett Smith	Harvey Peck	Wade Marvin Smith
1960–61	Harvey Peck	Robert Vernon Fulk Jr.	Howard Holderness Jr.	Raymond John Stanley
1961–62	Roger Babson Foushee	George Worth Campbell Jr.	Willis Padgett Whichard	Ray Simpson Farris Jr.
1962–63	Willis Padgett Whichard	Frederick Randolph Anderson Jr.	Hans Randolph Frankfort	no record
1963–64	Allen Thomson Cronenberg Jr.	Harold Thompson Mann	Harry Whitney Durand	Trawick Hamilton Stubbs Jr.
1964–65	Philip Augustine Baddour Jr.	Edward Stephens Martin	Heathcote Woolsey Wales	Roger William Smith
1965–66	Roger William Smith	Joseph Franklin Martin	Malvern Francis King Jr.	James Roy Fullwood
1966–67	Malvern Francis King Jr.	William Arthur Hays	Armistead Jones Maupin Jr.	James Roy Fullwood

Year	Jason	Hyparchos	Grammateus	Chrystopher
1967–68	Robert Carl Hunter	Charles Randolph Myer	Steven Alan Hockfield	William Propst Miller
1968–69	Steven Alan Hockfield	Warren Hal Schonfeld	Franklin St. Clair Clark	George West Krichbaum Jr.
1969–70	George West Krichbaum Jr.	Kenneth Coyner Day	James David Little	Charles Patrick Farris Jr.
1970–71	Peter Megargee Brown Jr.	Kenneth Coyner Day	J. Vincent Townsend III	John Patrick McDowell III
1971–72	Stephen Alexis LaTour	Paul Frederick Hoch Jr.	Peter Welles Hall	Peter Hafner Jost
1972–73	Stephen Alexis LaTour	Louis Joseph Loveland Jr.	Lawrence Alan Reid	William Barden Griffin
1973–74	Nancy Logan Haigwood	Allen Greene Mask Jr.	Reid Lloyd Phillips	Charles Frankling Miller
1974–75	Susan Anne Case	Murray Jules Fogler	Richard James Epps Jr.	Lee Lovell Corum
1975–76	Charles Thomas Humphrles	Walter Etheridge Daniels	Lisa Gayle Bradley	Thomas Roswell West
1976–77	Cathy Janis Rosenthal	Kathryn Newsome Campbell	John Dargon Watson	James Crawford Roberts Jr.
1977–78	Boyd Stephen Toben	Barry Lynn Smith	Paul Harold Arne	John Coleman Reid
1978–79	Samuel Thomas Sockwell	Isaac Byron Horton III	William Douglass Parmelee	Suzanne Mallary Mitchell
1979–80	Dana Lynn Cagle	Stephen Ward DeVine	Ann Mario Martinelli	William David Porterfield
1980–81	Ronald Gail Boatwright	Sharon Lee Parker	Jennifer Weiss	Robert Walter Saunders
1981–82	Joseph Moody Buckner	Robert Edward Johnson	Evelyn Ruth Leaver	Margaret Graham Leight
1982–83	Robert Edward Johnson	ElChino Miro Martin	Maxlyn LaVie Ellison	Nadine Marie Bourgeois
1983–84	Robert Joseph Bach	Stephen Alphonsus Mitchell	Julie Christine Chiu	Susan Elizabeth Walsh
1984–85	John Bernhardt Wilson Jr.	Timothy Patrick Sullivan	David Jeffrey Maslia	LaQuetta Ann Robinson
1985–86	Andrew James Balgarnie	Jack Edmunh Mohr	Jeremy Joshua Ofseyer	Mary Elizabeth Evans
1986–87	Camille Zebretta Roddy	Michael Roscoe Wilson	William Regan Burton	Mark Hersey Pavao
1987–88	Bryan Christopher Hassel	Emily Urquhart Ayscue	Janet Roach	Todd Christopher Hart
1988–89	Claude Ricketts Maechling	William Forest Yelverton II	Eileen Renee Carlton	Andrew Bennett Taubman
1989–90	Kent Stuart Hathaway Jr.	Clay Bernardin Thorp	Laurie Ann Winkler	Robert Cameron Cooke Jr.
1990–91	Timothy Quaid Karcher	Fitzgerald Clareforster Edwards	Lisa Lanette Frye	Ruth Tappan Dowling

Year	Jason	Hyparchos	Grammateus	Chrystopher
1991–92	Vann Donaldson	Jessica Leigh Vollmer	Elizabeth Gracie Abbot	Quaker Elizabeth Kappel
1992–93	Matthew Scott Peeler	Eric Dexter Ose	Mark Hayes Chilton	Christy Lynn Pons
1993–94	Felicia Eugenia Mebane	Eric Scott Montross	Kevin Sloane Moran	Caroline Bernice Philson
1994–95	James Davidson	George Edward Battle III	William Li-Goon Fan	Myles O'Hara Presler
1995–96	Nicholas S. MacPherson Johnston	Loura Elaine Edmisten	Michelle Lesley Johnson	John Howard Strickler
1996–97	Katherine Seton McNerney	Susanna Lovell Matsen	Timothy John Burke	Grace Chia-Lan Chu
1997–98	Scott Hunter Boze	Haralda Mavis Gragg	Kimberly Erin McCutcheon	George Lee Jackson
1998–99	Rebecca Erin Hockfield	Lacey Adele Hawthorne	Kimberly Erin McCutcheon	Kimberly Joy Gray
1999–2000	David Wayne Jernigan	Jeffrey Larkin Nieman	Amy Whaley	Ryan Schlitt
2000–01	Ali Alexander Mehfar	Allexandre Little	no record	Dennis Leonidas Markatos
2001–02	Eric David Johnson	Shawn Brooks	Emily McGlone Kathleen Hunter	Bharath Parthasarathy
2002–03	Scott Samuel Werry	Frederick William Hashagen III	Maneesha Agarwal	Karine Dube
2003–04	Leia Michelle Kelly	Rebecca Susanne Williford	Branson Halsted Page	Jonathan Philip Slain
2004–05	Conitras Mamieal Houston	Ashton Lee Wheeler	Erin Nicole Davis	Daniel Evan Waxman

Notes

Abbreviations

Records   Records of the Order of the Golden Fleece, University Archives, Louis Round Wilson Library, University of North Carolina at Chapel Hill, Chapel Hill, N.C.

MB   Minute Book

Preface

1. Order of the Golden Fleece Centennial Committee minutes, May 11 and May 18, 2002, Records.

2. Ibid., May 18, 2002.

3. Minutes, February 1 and June 4, 1922, Records.

4. Coulter, *History of the Golden Fleece*, preface.

5. Douglass Hunt to Michael G. Martin, April 3, 1987, Records.

6. See "The Golden Fleece," *Tar Heel*, June 1904; *Yackety Yack*, 1908, pp. 213–14; and John S. Cansler, "The Golden Fleece," *University Magazine*, November 1913, pp. 73–74.

7. "Resolution Authorizing a Public Address and a Public Book on the History of the Order of the Golden Fleece for the Years 1904 through 2004," October 21, 2003, Records.

Prologue

1. George Lensing and Kenneth Reckford, "Narration during Tapping Ceremony, Order of the Golden Fleece," 1993, Records.

Chapter One

1. House, *Light That Shines*, pp. 85–89.

2. Coates, *Edward Kidder Graham*, pp. 94–95.

3. House, *Light That Shines*, p. 86.

4. Snider, *Light on the Hill*, p. 245.

5. MB 1904–1911, p. 7, Records.

6. *Yackety Yack*, 1904, pp. 56–60; ibid., 1903, p. 23; Battle, *History of the University*, pp. 606, 614–15, 625, 747.

7. "The Golden Fleece," *Tar Heel*, June 1904.

8. MB 1904–1911, p. 7, Records.

9. "The Golden Fleece," *Tar Heel*, June 1904. See also John S. Cansler, "The Golden Fleece," *University Magazine*, November 1913, pp. 73–75.

10. *Yackety Yack*, 1904, pp. 19–27; Battle, *History of the University*, pp. 605, 630, 751.

11. *Yackety Yack*, 1904, p. 56.

12. Snider, *Light on the Hill*, p. 11; N.C. Laws 1789, ch. 20.

13. Snider, *Light on the Hill*, p. 141.

14. Battle, *History of the University*, p. 608; Wilson, *University of North Carolina*, p. 181.

15. Wilson, *Historical Sketches*, p. 30; Wilson, *University of North Carolina*, p. 55; Battle, *History of the University*, pp. 609–10.

16. Battle, *History of the University*, pp. 607–10.

17. House, *Light That Shines*, p. 8.

18. Snider, *Light on the Hill*, pp. 155–56.

19. House, *Light That Shines*, p. 8.

20. Wilson, *University of North Carolina*, p. 21.

21. Ibid., p. 22.

22. Coates, *Edward Kidder Graham*, p. 18.

23. Wilson, *University of North Carolina*, p. 23.

24. Battle, *History of the University*, p. 611; Wilson, *University of North Carolina*, p. 63.

25. Wilson, *University of North Carolina*, p. 22.

26. Battle, *History of the University*, p. 612.

27. House, *Light That Shines*, pp. 38–41.

28. Wilson, *University of North Carolina*, p. 23; *Yackety Yack*, 1904, pp. 151–71.

29. *Yackety Yack*, 1904, pp. 151–71; Wilson, *University of North Carolina*, pp. 25–26.

30. Wilson, *University of North Carolina*, p. 25; Jen Pilla, "The Ground Just Covered," *Daily Tar Heel*, February 23, 1993.

31. *Yackety Yack*, 1904.

32. Wilson, *University of North Carolina*, p. 25; *Yackety Yack*, 1904, pp. 147–48.

33. Coates, *Edward Kidder Graham*, p. 110.

34. Cansler, "Golden Fleece," p. 73.

35. Wilson, *University of North Carolina*, pp. 24–25.

36. Ibid., p. 152.

Chapter Two

1. Battle, *History of the University*, p. 626.

2. Wilson, *University of North Carolina*, pp. 179–81.

3. House, *Light That Shines*, p. 87.

4. Coates, *Edward Kidder Graham*, p. 27.

5. Coates to Professor Horace Williams, in *University of North Carolina Record*, January 1919, p. 8.

6. MB 1904–1911, pp. 7–9, Records.

7. Ibid., pp. 9–10.

8. Ibid., p. 13.

9. Wilson, *University of North Carolina*, pp. 54–55.

10. *Yackety Yack*, 1904, pp. 19–27, 54.

11. MB 1904–1911, p. 15, Records.

12. For further background, see Markale, *Templar Treasure at Gisors;* Read, *Templars;* and Burman, *Templars, Knights of God.*

13. MB 1904–1911, pp. 17–19, Records.

14. Ibid., pp. 21, 33, 37.

15. Ibid., p. 23.

16. See "Golden Fleece, Order of the," *Encyclopaedia Britannica.*

17. MB 1904–1911, pp. 25, 27, 29, 31, Records; Coulter, *History of the Golden Fleece*, note to appendix.

18. MB 1904–1911, pp. 39–41, Records.

19. Ibid., p. 7.

20. "The Golden Fleece," *Tar Heel*, June 1904. See also H. H. Williams, "Notes for Address to Golden Fleece, May 11, 1921," University of North Carolina Collection of Mounted Clippings, vol. 8, p. 2627, North Carolina Collection, Louis Round Wilson Library, University of North Carolina at Chapel Hill.

Chapter Three

1. MB 1904–1911, p. 39, Records; Young Men's Christian Association, *Student Handbook of the University of North Carolina*, 1904–1905, p. 16.

2. *Yackety Yack*, 1908, pp. 213–14.

3. John S. Cansler, "The Golden Fleece," *University Magazine*, November 1913, pp. 73–74.

4. The myths also appear in the *Tar Heel* on May 15, 1923, which reports that the order was proposed by Professor Alexander and was based on Yale University's Skull and Bones.

5. Coulter, *History of the Golden Fleece*, pp. 5–7.

6. Wilson, *University of North Carolina*, pp. 63–64, 152. Wilson also said that the members of the order "found it easier to become interested in the mysteries attending the rites of initiation than in laying a guiding hand upon student affairs" (153), a statement that overlooks the many active works of the order in its early years, which are described in chapter 6.

7. House, *Light That Shines*, p. 179; Snider, *Light on the Hill*, p. 146.

8. See George Lensing and Kenneth Reckford, "Golden Fleece—Introduction and Brief History, Following Tapping Ceremony," 1993, Records.

9. Coulter, *History of the Golden Fleece*, p. 5.

10. MB 1904–1911, pp. 7–9, Records.

11. Coates, *Edward Kidder Graham*, pp. 94–95; Coates to Professor Horace Williams, *University of North Carolina Record*, January 1919, p. 8.

12. House, *Light That Shines*, p. 179; see also the *Tar Heel*, November 23, 1905, which reports that at a banquet of the Golden Fleece on November 14, "Dr. Alexander, himself a member of the famous Yale Senior order, Skull and Bones, remarked that 'it gives me great pleasure to have such an opportunity to live again the life [I] used to live.'"

13. Eleanor Morris to G. Nicholas Herman, e-mail, June 21, 2004, Records.

14. Account given to the author by Argonaut Douglass Hunt. See also Douglass Hunt to Michael G. Martin, April 3, 1987, Records.

15. See John Sanders to Willis P. Whichard, Memorandum re: "Founding date, Order of the Golden Fleece," September 27, 2001, Records.

16. Technically, Phi Beta Kappa was preceded by a society of uncertain nature called the Flat Hat, which was founded in 1750 and existed for approximately twenty years. See Baird, *Baird's Manual*, p. 5.

17. See Hastings, *Phi Beta Kappa*. See also Edward E. Hale, "A Fossil from the Tertiary," *Atlantic Monthly* 44 (July 1879): 99.

18. Wilson, *University of North Carolina*, p. 23.

19. Robbins, *Secrets of the Tomb*, p. 3.

20. Ibid., pp. 3, 82–84.

21. The Fleece also has little in common with the two other senior societies at Yale, Scroll and Key and Wolf's Head, founded in 1842 and 1883, respectively. These secret, largely fraternal societies were founded as alternatives to or imitations of Skull and Bones and are said to have had the early effect of "emphasiz[ing] class divisions as a centerpiece of the Yale experience." Robbins, *Secrets of the Tomb*, pp. 38, 53, 63.

22. 1913 Constitution, art. II, Records.

23. By-laws of the Order of the Golden Fleece, art. III, Records.

24. John Morgan (executive director of the Omicron Delta Kappa Society, Inc.), interview by G. Nicholas Herman, October 2003, Omicron Delta Kappa Society National Headquarters, University of Kentucky, Lexington, Kentucky. One of the founding faculty advisors of ODK was Washington and Lee University's president, Henry Louis Smith, who had received an honorary Doctor of Laws degree from the University of North Carolina in 1906. Grant, *Alumni History*, p. 753; Battle, *History of the University*, p. 656. But there is no evidence that Smith knew anything about the Order of the Golden Fleece prior to 1914. In 1924, he was the featured speaker at the order's tapping ceremony. Coulter, *History of the Golden Fleece*, p. 21.

25. Latture, "Beginning of ODK."

26. Coulter, *History of the Golden Fleece*, p. 30. See also "The Driftwood Fire," *Tar Heel*, December 11, 1926, and Minutes of November 21, 1926, Records. In 1938, *Cap and Gown*, the yearbook for the University of the South in Sewanee, Tennessee, requested the right to use the name of the Golden Fleece to establish a

chapter of the order at that university. The Fleece turned down this proposal, as well. Coulter, *History of the Golden Fleece*, p. 36.

27. Omicron Delta Kappa, *Manual*, pp. 59–64.

Chapter Four

1. 1913 Constitution, art. II, Records. Although the 1904 Constitution has been lost, various amendments to the Constitution discussed in the order's minute books of 1904–1911 and 1913–1927 indicate that the differences between the 1904 and 1913 constitutions relate to technical, procedural matters rather than to the order's fundamental purposes and qualifications for membership.

2. Ibid., art. V.

3. 1994 Constitution, art. III, Records. See also 1981 Constitution, art. II and art. V, sec. 4, Records.

4. Roster of the Order of the Golden Fleece, 1981, Records.

5. *Tar Heel*, May 9, 1911; April 30, 1914; April 8, 1915; April 29, 1916; April 14, 1917; April 13, 1918; and May 2, 1919.

6. Ibid., April 2, 1920.

7. Ibid., May 10 and 13, 1921.

8. Wilson, *Historical Sketches*, p. 36.

9. Minutes of February 26 and March 8, 1911, Records.

10. Snider, *Light on the Hill*, p. 167.

11. Minutes of January 16, 1921, Records.

12. Coates, *Edward Kidder Graham*, pp. 54, 57.

13. "Golden Fleece to Tap Best Men on Campus," *Tar Heel*, May 9, 1922.

14. *Daily Tar Heel*, April 27, 1933.

15. *Yackety Yack*, 1924, p. 86.

16. "Fuz" was later spelled "Fuzz." See *Tar Heel*, May 3, 1924.

17. *Tar Heel*, May 13 and 16, 1924.

18. Coulter, *History of the Golden Fleece*, pp. 21–23.

19. *Tar Heel*, May 6, 1926.

20. Minutes of November 21, 1926, Records. See also "The Driftwood Fire," *Tar Heel*, December 11, 1926.

21. Minutes of November 22, 1926, Records.

22. See "Golden Fleece," *Tar Heel*, December 9, 1926.

23. Minutes of December 3, 1926, Records.

24. *Tar Heel*, December 9, 1926.

25. Ibid.

26. Ibid., December 11, 1926.

27. Ibid., December 9, 1926.

28. Coates and Coates, *Story of Student Government*, p. 427.

29. *Tar Heel*, January 20, 1927, emphasis mine.

30. Ibid.

31. Ibid., May 10, 1928.

32. Ibid., May 17, 1928.

33. 1913 Constitution, art. V, Records. On changing selection criteria, compare Minutes of May 25, 1913, wherein it was emphasized that selection of new members should not be based simply on "one outstanding distinction or attainment," with Minutes of April 28, 1909, and April 25, 1910, wherein the order emphasized different categories of student service in making selections. Records.

34. Coulter, *History of the Golden Fleece*, p. 35.

35. 1913 Constitution (before amendment), art. V, sec. 2, Records.

36. Undated Minutes of May 1913, Records.

37. 1981 Constitution, art. V, sec. 1; 1994 By-Laws, art. XI, secs. 2 and 3, both in Records. As a matter of practice, the Fleece has also selected honorary members who, though they have not contributed directly to undergraduate student life, exemplify the highest ideals of the order.

38. See 1981 Constitution, art. V, sec. 2, Records.

39. Historical comments of George Lensing, September 2004, Records.

40. Coates and Coates, *Story of Student Government*, p. 254.

41. Report of Argonaut Tom Lambeth, 1957–1958, p. 3, Records.

42. Stephen A. LaTour, "Order of the Golden Fleece, University of North Carolina at Chapel Hill, Information for the Historical Record of the Order," April 2003, Records. See also Coates and Coates, *Story of Student Government*, p. 256.

43. 1994 Constitution, art. III, Records.

Chapter Five

1. MB 1904–1911, pp. 33–37, Records.

2. Coulter, *History of the Golden Fleece*, p. 7. See also MB 1904–1911, p. 23, Records.

3. Minutes of March 5, 1905; 1913 Constitution, art. XI; 1981 Constitution, art. X, all in Records.

4. Preston Epps to Gladys Hall Coates, April 11, 1969, Records.

5. 1981 Constitution, art. V, sec. 2; 1994 Constitution, art. IV, sec. 3; 1994 By-Laws, art. IV, sec. 3, all in Records.

6. Coulter, *History of the Golden Fleece*, pp. 9, 18; Minutes of May 2, 1905, Records; 1913 Constitution, art. V, sec. VI, Records.

7. Coulter, *History of the Golden Fleece*, pp. 13, 18. See also Minutes of April 15, 1905, Records.

8. The order first discussed a public tapping ceremony in 1908. See Minutes of June 1, 1908, Records.

9. On the ribbons, see 1913 Constitution, art. XI, sec. 3; 1981 Constitution, art. X; 1994 By-Laws, art. XV, sec. 1, all in Records. For the ceremony, see Coulter, *History of the Golden Fleece*, pp. 10–11.

10. Minutes of April 3, 1919, Records; Coulter, *History of the Golden Fleece*, pp. 13–14.

11. Coulter, *History of the Golden Fleece*, pp. 13–14.

12. *Tar Heel*, April 2, 1920.

13. Coulter, *History of the Golden Fleece*, pp. 19–20.

14. The keynote speakers for 1921 through 1935 were Professor Horace Williams (1921); Cameron Morrison, governor of North Carolina (1922 and 1927); John Johnston Parker, judge of the U.S. Court of Appeals for the Fourth Circuit (1923 and 1931); Henry Louis Smith, president of Washington and Lee University (1924); Edward Mims, professor and head of the English Department at Vanderbilt University (1925); James Howard E. Rondthaler, president of Salem College (1926); Francis P. Gaines, president of Wake Forest University (1928); Oliver Max Gardner, governor of North Carolina (1929); Harry Woodburn Chase, president of the University of North Carolina (1930); Henry L. Stevens, national commander of the American Legion (1932); John Christoph Blucher Ehringhaus, governor of North Carolina (1933); A. H. "Sandy" Graham, lieutenant governor of North Carolina (1934); and Clyde R. Hoey, editor of the *Cleveland Star* (1935).

15. Historical summary by William H. Miller, Records. See also John Sanders to G. Nicholas Herman, memorandum re: "Fleece emblem and Foundation," August 10, 2003, Records.

16. Coulter, *History of the Golden Fleece*, pp. 33–34.

17. George Lensing, "Introduction to Order of Golden Fleece Tapping Ceremony," 1992, Records.

18. When Parker was invited to join the order as a student, he declined. Subsequently, he was tapped as an honorary member in 1923 and again in 1949. Coulter, *History of the Golden Fleece*, p. 19.

19. See Alexander Heard, 1989 Frank Porter Graham Lecture; Richard Allen Vinroot, "Profiles in Excellence," 1993 Frank Porter Graham Lecture; Willis P. Whichard, 1992 Frank Porter Graham Lecture; Doris W. Betts, 2001 Frank Porter Graham Lecture (reproduced on the Golden Fleece website, www.unc.edu/ogf), all in Records. Keynote speakers at the tapping ceremonies from 1958 through 2004 were Clifton Leonard Moore, associate justice of the N.C. Supreme Court (1958); Albert Coates, professor of law and founder of the UNC-CH Institute of Government (1960); Terry Sanford, governor of North Carolina and later president of Duke University (1961, 1968, and 1987); Charles Bishop Kuralt, CBS news reporter (1969 and 1980); Thomas Grey Wicker, member of the editorial staff of the *New York Times* (1970); L. Richardson Preyer, U.S. congressman for North Carolina (1971 and 1981); William Davis Snider, editor of the *Greensboro Daily News* (1972); James Bryan McMillan Sr., U.S. district court judge (1973); Julius Levonne Chambers, chancellor of North Carolina Central University (1974, 1991, and 1997); Howard Nathaniel Lee, mayor of Chapel Hill and later member of the N.C. Senate (1975); Hamilton Harris Hobgood, N.C. superior court judge (1977); Samuel R. Williamson, professor at UNC-CH and later vice-chancellor of the University of the South (1978); John McNeill Smith Jr., prominent attorney and former member of the N.C. Senate (1979); Hargrove "Skipper" Bowles Jr., former member of the N.C. House of Representatives and N.C. Senate (1982); James Baxter Hunt Jr., governor

of North Carolina (1983); James Hayes Shofner Cooper, U.S. congressman for Tennessee (1984); Dean E. Smith, UNC-CH basketball coach (1985); James R. Leutze, chancellor of UNC-Wilmington (1986); A. Anson Dorrance IV, UNC-CH soccer coach (1988); George Alexander Heard, chancellor emeritus of Vanderbilt University (1989); Judith A. Hines, prominent pioneer in social work (1990); Willis Padgett Whichard, associate justice of the N.C. Supreme Court and later dean of the Norman Adrian Wiggins School of Law at Campbell University (1992); Richard Allen Vinroot, mayor of Charlotte, North Carolina (1993); Marie Watters Colton, first woman speaker pro tem of the N.C. House of Representatives (1994); Chuck S. Stone Jr., professor of journalism at UNC-CH (1995); Shelby Dade Foote, historian of the American Civil War (1996); Edwin M. Yoder Jr., Pulitzer Prize–winning editor (1998); Erskine Boyce Bowles, White House chief of staff to President William Jefferson Clinton (1999); Benjamin S. Ruffin, first African American chairman of the University of North Carolina Board of Governors (2000); Doris Waugh Betts, novelist and professor of English at UNC-CH (2001); Richard Judson Richardson, professor of political science and provost at UNC-CH (2002); Robert G. Kirkpatrick Jr., professor of English at UNC-CH (2003); and Francis S. Collins, director of the National Human Genome Research Institute (2004).

20. The tradition is codified in the order's 1981 and 1994 Constitutions. See 1981 Constitution, art. IX, sec. 2; 1994 Constitution, art. IX, Sec. 2, both in Records.

21. See Coulter, *History of the Golden Fleece*, p. 29; Minutes of March 10, 1916, Records.

22. In some years, the banquet has been held at the George Watts Hill Alumni Center or at the Dean E. Smith Center.

23. E. Osborne Ayscue Jr., "My Recollections of the Order of the Golden Fleece," March 27, 2003, Records. See also George Lensing, Historical comments, September 2004, Records. At the graduation breakfast in May 1980, Preston Herschel Epps, a professor of Greek at UNC-CH who was unable to attend the event, submitted short remarks entitled "True Freedom Also Binds," which were read to the breakfast gathering and were subsequently published in the May 19, 1980, edition of the *Chapel Hill Newspaper*.

24. See Lenoir Chambers, "Excellence in a Democracy," May 16, 1959; Fred H. Weaver, "The Changing University and the Constant Ideal," March 29, 1965; Douglass Hunt, "Remarks to the Order of the Golden Fleece," April 9, 1976, and April 15, 1981, all in Records. Among those who gave formal banquet addresses were Lenoir Chambers, editor of the *Norfolk Virginia Pilot* (1959); Douglass Hunt, vice chancellor for administration at UNC-CH (1964, 1976, and 1981); Frederick Henry Weaver, dean of students at UNC-CH and later vice-president of the University of North Carolina (1965); James Clarence Wallace, teacher at N.C. State University and mayor of Chapel Hill (1971); Samuel Smythe Hill Jr., professor of religious studies at UNC-CH (1972); Walter Smith Spearman, professor of journalism at UNC-CH (1973 and 1977); and William Brantley Aycock, chancellor emeritus of UNC-CH (1978).

25. Coulter, *History of the Golden Fleece*, p. 36.

26. 1994 Constitution, art. IV, sec. 3; 1994 By-Laws, art. IV, sec. 3, both in Records.

27. Coulter, *History of the Golden Fleece*, p. 37. Before 1949, the idea of publishing a complete roster of Argonauts was considered in 1911, 1927, and 1937. See Minutes of May 3, 1911, and May 26, 1927, in Records. See also Blue Books of 1962, 1968, 1981, 1994, 1999, and 2004 in Records.

28. See Order of the Golden Fleece Jason's Handbook, 1994, Records. The website, at <http://www.unc.edu/ogf>, was originally designed by Argonaut Manali Indravadan Patel. See Eric D. Johnson, Historical report to G. Nicholas Herman, Records.

29. Coulter, *History of the Golden Fleece*, p. 20.

30. See Stephen A. LaTour, "Order of the Golden Fleece, University of North Carolina at Chapel Hill, Information for the Historical Record of the Order," April 2003, Records.

31. 1981 Constitution, art. IX, sec. 2, Records.

32. See, for example, 1913 Constitution, art. XII, Records.

33. Coulter, *History of the Golden Fleece*, p. 36.

34. Ibid., pp. 36–37.

35. Robert E. Johnson to Argonauts, July 1983, Records.

36. John Sanders to G. Nicholas Herman, memorandum re: "Fleece emblem and Foundation," August 10, 2003; Articles of Incorporation of Golden Fleece Foundation, Inc., 1983; By-Laws of the Golden Fleece Foundation, 1983 and 1988, all in Records.

37. Jason's Handbook, 1983; Robert E. Johnson to Argonauts, July 1983, both in Records.

38. Account given to the author by Argonaut Douglass Hunt.

39. October 21, 2003, Amendment to 1994 By-Laws at art. V, sec. 4, Records.

40. Ibid. at art. XIII.

Chapter Six

1. "The Golden Fleece," *Tar Heel*, June 1904.

2. *Tar Heel*, November 16, 1904.

3. Minutes of November 10, 1904, Records.

4. At a meeting on November 11, 1904, the order asked Argonaut Frank McLean, editor-in-chief of the *Tar Heel*, and Roach Sidney Stewart to explain to the paper the order's position in "the Soph-Med Affair." Minutes of November 11, 1904, Records.

5. *Tar Heel*, November 16, 1904.

6. 1913 Constitution, art. IV ("The affairs of the society should be secret except in regard to its general aims and ideals"); 1994 Constitution, art. XII ("Traditionally, all meetings of the Active Order and involvement in campus affairs are conducted in secret"), both in Records.

7. Coulter, *History of the Golden Fleece*, p. 9.

8. Minutes of November 14, 1904, Records; *Tar Heel*, November 23, 1904.

9. Coates and Coates, *Story of Student Government*, pp. 142–43.

10. Snider, *Light on the Hill*, p. 152.

11. Minutes of November 11 and 14, 1904, Records; Wilson, *University of North Carolina*, p. 153; *Tar Heel*, November 30, 1904.

12. *Tar Heel*, November 30, 1904.

13. Quoted in Battle, *History of the University*, pp. 698–99.

14. Minutes of September 15, 1905, Records.

15. The suggested rules were that freshmen: "(1) stop smoking cigars; (2) not loaf in the post office; (3) keep off the grass; (4) wear brown caps on weekdays; (5) not wear prep school medals and pins." Minutes of November 7, 1905, Records.

16. Minutes of November 21, 1905, Records.

17. *Tar Heel*, October 26, 1905.

18. Wilson, *University of North Carolina*, pp. 154–55; Coates and Coates, *Story of Student Government*, pp. 143–46.

19. Wilson, *University of North Carolina*, pp. 156–59; Coates and Coates, *Story of Student Government*, pp. 146–50; Snider, *Light on the Hill*, p. 153.

20. Coates and Coates, *Story of Student Government*, p. 150.

21. Ibid., pp. 151–52; Coates, *What the University*, p. 43.

22. Coates and Coates, *Story of Student Government*, p. 152. As a further unifying measure, in late 1917, the order proposed to President Graham that the heads of the different campus organizations come up with a schedule of all organization meetings and activities to be published in the *Tar Heel*. With ten social fraternities and over twenty non-frat organizations, the Fleece believed that making public the various activities of these organizations would make them more transparent and help bind the student body together. Beginning with its December 22, 1917, edition, the *Tar Heel* published these organization activity schedules on a regular basis. See Minutes of October 22 and December 3, 1917, and January 7 and February 18, 1918, Records.

23. *Tar Heel*, September 28, 1917.

24. Coulter, *History of the Golden Fleece*, p. 31.

25. William H. Miller, Historical report, Records.

26. Julian D. Mason Jr., Historical report, Records.

27. George R. Ragsdale, Historical report, Records.

28. Macon G. Patton and George R. Ragsdale, letter to the editor, *Daily Tar Heel*, November 26, 1957.

29. Coates and Coates, *Story of Student Government*, pp. 334–37, 345–61.

30. Humphries to G. Nicholas Herman, e-mail, January 12, 2004, Records.

31. Coates and Coates, *Story of Student Government*, pp. 360–61. See also James O. Cansler, letter, September 14, 1977, in folder "Student Affairs, Division of: 1976–77," Records of the Office of the Chancellor, Nelson Ferebee Taylor Series, 1972–1980, 40023, box 43.

32. 1913 Constitution, art. IX, sec. 2; 1981 Constitution, art. IX, sec. 1; 1994 Constitution, art. X, sec. 1, all in Records.

33. Jason's Minutes of 1958–1959; Raymond Taylor to William C. Friday, November 18 and 21, 1958; Friday to Raymond Taylor, October 21 and November 5, 1958; Thomas C. Creasy Jr. to Raymond Taylor, October 8, 1958; George Krichbaum, Historical report; Peter Brown, 1970–1971 Report to Argonauts; Stephen Alexis LaTour, Historical report; "Report of September 14, 1973 Meeting with Dr. James Taylor, SHS"; Nancy L. Haigwood to Chancellor Ferebee Taylor, February 18, 1974; Richard T. Stevens to Chancellor Ferebee Taylor, February 25, 1974; Ann Martinelli to the Chancellor's Search Committee, October 25, 1979; Minutes of October 21, 2003, and February 2 and 14, 2004, all in Records.

Chapter Seven

1. Douglass Hunt to Dr. Alexander Heard, March 4, 1989, Records.

2. *Daily Tar Heel*, April 28, 1953.

3. Julian Mason, interview by G. Nicholas Herman, July 1, 2004.

4. "Citation of Frank Porter Graham as Argonaut of the Half Century," retyped letter from Douglass Hunt to the Jason, March 6, 1953, Records. Graham was originally tapped into the order in 1908 as Argonaut number 40. He was first retapped in 1950. After the tapping ceremony, at which Graham was tapped for the third time, he joined the Fleece alumni at a reception at the Carolina Inn, where he was presented with a newly bound first edition of Jefferson Davis's two-volume *Rise and Fall of the Confederate Government*. The plaque he received bore the inscription "He hath showed thee, O man, what is good; and what doth the Lord require of thee, but to do justly, and to love mercy, and to walk humbly with thy God?"

5. Argonaut Frank Weston Fenhagen, interview by G. Nicholas Herman, July 14, 2004.

6. See Ashby, *Frank Porter Graham;* Ehle, *Dr. Frank;* and Pleasants and Burns, *Frank Porter Graham*.

7. "A Memorial Service for Allard Kenneth Lowenstein, Class of 1949," Memorial Hall, the University of North Carolina at Chapel Hill, April 21, 1980, p. 11 (remarks of Lindsay Tate, quoting Frank Porter Graham's "The Faith and Hope of America"), Records.

8. Alexander Heard (Argonaut 318), "The Frank Porter Graham Lecture on Excellence," tapping banquet of the Order of the Golden Fleece, April 7, 1989, Records.

Chapter Eight

1. Link, *William Friday*, pp. 204–5.

2. *Dickson v. Sitterson*, 280 F. Supp. 486, 498–99 (1968).

3. N.C. Gen. Stat. secs. 116–199 through 116–200 (1963).

4. Link, *William Friday*, p. 205.

5. Billingsley, *Communists on Campus*, pp. 3, 26–38.

8. Office of the University Registrar, "Summary of Changes in Headcount Enrollment," North Carolina Collection.

9. G. Nicholas Herman and Harriet Sugar, "A Proposal for the 1977–1978 Order of the Golden Fleece to Establish an Endowment for Funding an Undergraduate Scholarship for Freshman Minority Students at the University of North Carolina at Chapel Hill," October 6, 1977, Records.

10. G. Nicholas Herman to Mr. Hunt, handwritten note, October 14, 1977; Jason B. Stephen Toben to fellow Argonauts, November 14, 1977, both in Records.

11. Jason B. Stephen Toben to fellow Argonauts, April 27, 1978; Douglass Hunt to Professor George Lensing Jr. (faculty advisor, the Order of the Golden Fleece), memo re: the Lowenstein Scholarship Fund, September 4, 1987, both in Records.

12. Jason B. Stephen Toben to fellow Argonauts, November 14, 1977, Records.

13. Ibid., April 27, 1978, Records.

14. Hunt to Lensing, memo re: the Lowenstein Scholarship Fund, September 4, 1987, Records. The decision to name the scholarship in the name of Allard K. Lowenstein was reaffirmed by the order in 1988. Minutes of March 22, 1988, Records.

15. Shirley Ort, response to June 5, 2004, e-mail from G. Nicholas Herman, Records.

Chapter Ten

1. "A Memorial Service for Allard Kenneth Lowenstein, Class of 1949," Memorial Hall, the University of North Carolina at Chapel Hill, April 21, 1980, Records. The speakers were Argonauts James Clarence Wallace, John Lassiter Sanders, Banks Cooper Talley Jr., Richard James Murphy, Wade Marvin Smith, and Douglass Hunt, as well as Charles M. Jones, Lindsay Tate, and Brent McKnight.

2. Ibid., pp. 7, 22.

3. Ibid., pp. 7, 10, 17.

4. Ibid., p. 17.

5. Ibid., pp. 8–9. For books about Lowenstein's life, see Chafe, *Never Stop Running;* Cummings, *Pied Piper;* Harris, *Dreams Die Hard;* and Stone and Lowenstein, *Lowenstein.*

6. As Argonaut Edwin Milton Yoder Jr. put it, "Wallace had died before his time, of a few too many wee drams of the elixir his Scottish forebears brought to America." See "Remembering an Instructor, Leader in North Carolina," *News and Observer*, December 18, 1991.

7. "A Memorial Service for James Clarence Wallace, Class of 1944," Gerrard Hall, the University of North Carolina at Chapel Hill, 4:00 P.M., Sunday, December 8, 1991, Records. Argonauts who spoke at the service included John Lassiter Sanders, Joel Lawrence Fleishman, Edwin Milton Yoder Jr., Thomas Willis Lambeth, Eli Nachamson Evans, Nelson Ferebee Taylor, Jonathan Broome Howes, Norwood Eason Bryan Jr., and Douglass Hunt. The other speakers at the service were Clayton Stalnaker, Robert E. Seymour, Robert L. Epting, and Jerry Davidoff (in absentia).

8. Ibid., pp. 1, 29–30.

9. Ibid., pp. 1, 5.

10. Ibid., pp. 1, 15–16, 26, 32.

11. Ibid., pp. 3, 29, 31.

12. Ibid., pp. 8–9.

13. See prologue.

14. Jason James Davidson to Argonauts, 1995, Records.

15. Gordon Gray, president of the consolidated university from 1950–1955, became a Fleece member in 1929.

16. Citation for George Lensing Jr., Argonaut number 1026, Records.

17. Citation for Eleanor Saunders Morris, Argonaut number 1304, Records.

18. See Coates and Coates, *Story of Student Government*, pp. 291–313.

19. These addresses were given in 1964, 1976, and 1981. See Douglass Hunt, "Remarks to the Order of the Golden Fleece," April 19, 1976, and April 15, 1981, Records.

Chapter Eleven

1. Handwritten notes by John L. Sanders on "Golden Fleece Centenary," June 20, 2000, Records.

2. Ibid., May 19, 2001, Records.

3. Other members of the committee from 2000 through 2004 included Karine Dube, Carl Edgar Ervin, Frank Weston Fenhagen, Rosalind Runae Fuse-Hall, G. Nicholas Herman, Judith Ann Albergotti Hines, Conitras Mamieal Houston, Douglass Hunt, Nicholas Simon M. Johnston, George Lensing Jr., William Woodard McLendon, Eleanor Saunders Morris, Branson Halsted Page, Barath Parthasarathy, Jane Bethel Preyer, John Lassiter Sanders, Mark Howard Shelburne, Jonathan Philip Slain, Banks Cooper Talley Jr., Clay Bernardin Thorp, and Ashton Lee Wheeler.

4. Order of the Golden Fleece Centennial Committee minutes of October 11, 2001; John Sanders to Willis P. Whichard, memorandum re: "Founding date, Order of the Golden Fleece," September 27, 2001, both in Records.

5. "Report of the Centennial Committee's program subcommittee of Johnston, Herman, Lensing, and Werry about a potential program for the March 26–27 Centennial Celebration," Records.

6. Order of the Golden Fleece Centennial Committee minutes of May 11 and May 18, 2002, Records.

7. All centennial events were recorded on videotapes, which are preserved in the Fleece records in the University Archives at Louis Round Wilson Library. The events were also well publicized. See "Having Dared to Surpass the Many," *Carolina Alumni Review* 93, no. 2 (March/April 2004), p. 15; "Geneticist Collins' Speech, Age-Old ceremony on Tap as Golden Fleece Marks 100 Years," *UNC News Release—Carolina News Services*, no. 144, March 18, 2004; "UNC Order Tried to Ease Frat-Nonfrat Enmity," *Raleigh News and Observer*, March 22, 2004; "Argonauts Celebrate 100 Years," *Chapel Hill News*, March 24, 2004; "Golden Fleece Marking

100 Years," *Chapel Hill Herald*, March 24, 2004; "Historic Order Celebrates 100 Years," *Daily Tar Heel*, March 24, 2004; "Golden Service Brought to Light," *Daily Tar Heel*, March 25, 2004; "Fleece Unites Past, Present," *Daily Tar Heel*, March 26, 2004; and "The Golden Road," *Daily Tar Heel*, March 29, 2004.

8. "Centennial Celebration of the Order of the Golden Fleece, University of North Carolina at Chapel Hill: Introduction of Francis S. Collins, MD '77, PhD, as the Frank Porter Graham Lecturer," Hill Hall, Friday, March 26, 2004, Records.

9. Francis S. Collins, "Excellence: Four Characteristics and a Consequence," Frank Porter Graham Lecture on Excellence, 100th Anniversary of the Order of the Golden Fleece, the University of North Carolina at Chapel Hill, March 26, 2004, Records.

10. Rebecca Williford, Announcement of Argonaut of the Second Half-Century, March 27, 2004, Records.

11. See Link, *William Friday;* King, *Multicampus University of North Carolina.*

12. See also "The Golden Road," *Daily Tar Heel*, March 29, 2004.

13. Argonauts Joel Lawrence Fleishman and Thomas Willis Lambeth moderated the panel, which also included Phillip Leroy Clay, Rebecca Erin Hockfield, Eric David Johnson, Charles Batcheller Neely Jr., Howard Nathaniel Lee, J. Dickson Phillips Jr., and Sallie Shuping Russell.

14. See "1904–2004, Order of the Golden Fleece, 100 Years: Directory of Participants," Records.

Chapter Twelve

1. Battle, *History of the University*, p. 637.

2. See John S. Cansler, "The Golden Fleece," *University Magazine*, November 1913, p. 74.

3. "The Golden Fleece," *Tar Heel*, June 1904.

4. 1913 Constitution, art. V; 1981 Constitution, art. II and art. V, sec. 4; 1994 Constitution, art. III, all in Records.

5. These are Eben Alexander Residence Hall, William B. Aycock Family Medicine Center, Herman G. Baity Environmental Laboratory, Walter Reece Berryhill Hall, Hargrove Bowles Jr. Building, Kenneth M. Brinkhous Building, Dudley D. Carroll Hall, Harry Woodburn Chase Hall, Albert and Gladys Coates Building, Walter Royal Davis Library, John C. B. Ehringhaus Residence Hall, Robert Allison Fetzer Gymnasium, Christopher C. Fordham Hall, William and Ida Friday Center for Continuing Education, O. Max Gardner Hall, Frank Porter Graham Student Union, Frank Porter Graham Child Development Center, Edward Kidder Graham Memorial, Paul E. Green Theatre, Bernard George Greenberg Hall, Robert March Hanes Hall, Robert B. House Undergraduate Library, J. Harold Lineberger and Henry A. Lineberger Cancer Research Center, William W. McLendon Clinical Laboratories at UNC Hospitals, John Motley Morehead Building, John Motley Morehead Instructional Laboratory, Morehead Planetarium, Morehead-Patterson Bell Tower (for John Motley Morehead), Howard W. Odum Village, John J. Parker Residence

Hall, Knapp-Sanders School of Government (for John L. Sanders), Joseph Carlyle Sitterson Hall, Dean E. Smith Student Activities Center, Sonja Haynes Stone Center for Black Culture and History, Isaac M. Taylor Hall, Nelson Ferebee Taylor Reading Room in Davis Library, Claude Edward Teague Residence Hall, Van Hecke-Wettach Hall (for Maurice T. Van Hecke), Louis Round Wilson Library, Nathan Anthony Womack Clinical Sciences Building, Charles T. Woollen Gymnasium, the Horace Williams Airport, and Horace Williams House. See Rachael Long, Building Notes, University of North Carolina at Chapel Hill, 1993, North Carolina Collection.

Bibliography

Archival Sources

Chapel Hill, N.C.
Louis Round Wilson Library, University of North Carolina at Chapel Hill
North Carolina Collection
University Archives
Records of the Office of the Chancellor
Nelson Ferebee Taylor Series, 1972–1980
Records of the Order of the Golden Fleece

Published Sources

Ashby, Warren. *Frank Porter Graham: A Southern Liberal*. Winston-Salem: J. F. Blair, 1980.

Baird, William Raimond. *Baird's Manual of American College Fraternities*. Edited by John Robson. 19th edition. Menasha, Wisc.: Baird's Manual Foundation, 1977.

Battle, Kemp P. *History of the University of North Carolina from 1868 to 1912*. Volume 2 of *History of the University of North Carolina*. Raleigh: Printed for the author by Edwards and Broughton, 1912.

Billingsley, William J. *Communists on Campus: Race, Politics, and the Public University in Sixties North Carolina*. Athens: University of Georgia Press, 1999.

Burman, Edward. *The Templars: Knights of God*. Rochester, Vt.: Destiny Books, 1986.

Chafe, William Henry. *Never Stop Running: Allard Lowenstein and the Struggle to Save American Liberalism*. New York: Basic Books, 1993.

Coates, Albert. *Edward Kidder Graham, Harry Woodburn Chase, Frank Porter Graham: Three Men in the Transition of the University of North Carolina at Chapel Hill from a Small College to a Great University*. [Chapel Hill]: Privately printed, 1988.

———. *What the University of North Carolina Meant to Me: A Report to the Chancellors and Presidents and to the People with Whom I Have Lived and Worked from 1916 to 1969*. Richmond: William Byrd Press, 1969.

Coates, Albert, and Gladys Hall Coates. *The Story of Student Government in the University of North Carolina at Chapel Hill.* Chapel Hill: Professor Emeritus Fund, 1985.

Coulter, William Robert. *History of the Golden Fleece, 1903–1950.* Chapel Hill: Order of the Golden Fleece, 1950.

Cummings, Richard. *The Pied Piper: Allard K. Lowenstein and the Liberal Dream.* New York: Grove Press, 1985.

Ehle, John. *Dr. Frank: Life with Frank Porter Graham.* Chapel Hill: Franklin Street Books, 1993.

Grant, Daniel Lindsey. *Alumni History of the University of North Carolina.* 2nd edition. Durham: Christian and King, 1924.

Harris, David. *Dreams Die Hard: Three Men's Journey through the Sixties.* New York: St. Martin's, 1982.

Hastings, William T. *Phi Beta Kappa as a Secret Society.* Washington, D.C.: United Chapters of Phi Beta Kappa, 1965.

House, Robert B. *The Light that Shines: Chapel Hill, 1912–1916.* Chapel Hill: University of North Carolina Press, 1964.

King, Arnold K. *The Multicampus University of North Carolina Comes of Age, 1956–1986.* Chapel Hill: University of North Carolina, 1987.

Latture, Rupert N. "The Beginning of ODK." *The Circle* 59, no. 2 (Winter 1980).

Link, William A. "William Friday and the North Carolina Speaker Ban Crisis, 1963–1968." *North Carolina Historical Review* 72, no. 2 (April 1995): 198–228.

——. *William Friday: Power, Purpose, and American Higher Education.* Chapel Hill: University of North Carolina Press, 1995.

Markale, Jean. *The Templar Treasure at Gisors.* Rochester, Vt.: Inner Traditions, 2003.

Omicron Delta Kappa Society. *Omicron Delta Kappa Manual of the National Leadership Honor Society, 2000–2002.* Lexington, KY: Omicron Delta Kappa Society, 2002.

Pleasants, Julian, and Augustus M. Burns III. *Frank Porter Graham and the 1950 Senate Race in North Carolina.* Chapel Hill: University of North Carolina Press, 1990.

Read, Piers Paul. *The Templars.* New York: St. Martin's, 1999.

Robbins, Alexandra. *Secrets of the Tomb: Skull and Bones, the Ivy League, and the Hidden Paths of Power.* Boston: Little, Brown, 2002.

Snider, William D. *Light on the Hill: A History of the University of North Carolina at Chapel Hill.* Chapel Hill: University of North Carolina Press, 1992.

Stone, Gregory, and Douglas Lowenstein, eds. *Lowenstein: Acts of Courage and Belief.* San Diego: Harcourt Brace, 1983.

Wilson, Louis Round. *Louis Round Wilson's Historical Sketches.* Durham: Moore Publishing, 1976.

——. *The University of North Carolina, 1900–1930: The Making of a Modern University.* Chapel Hill: University of North Carolina Press, 1957.

Index

Page numbers in italic text refer to illustrations. OGF stands for the Order of the Golden Fleece.